ON TO THE SHOW

Fort Wayne's lasting impact on the NHL and the hockey world

BY BLAKE SEBRING

DEDICATION

For Linda Anderson, who helps put so many things into perspective.

Cover and book design by Angel Knuth

Edited by Melody Schmitt-Foreman

Thanks to Mike and Laura Stuckey, Tom Miracle, Mike Emrick, Wes McCauley, the Wallenstein family, Dave and Sheryl Krieg, Ruth and Ken Wiegmann, Con Madigan, John Torchetti, Bruce and Crystal Boudreau, John Anderson, Fred Knipscheer, Rob Laird, Robbie Irons, Kevin Kaminski, Mike Butters, Steve and Barb Wissman, Joe Franke, Angel Knuth, Natalie Zehr, Melody Schmitt-Foreman, Terry Purinton, Kevin Weekes, Alton White, Brandon Faber, Eddie and Gayle Long, Len and Martha Thornson, Chuck Bailey, Shane Albahrani, Larry Schmitt, Betty Stein, Chad and Susanne Higgins, Rick and Lisa Tomlinson, Eric and Trina Eastin, Beth Behrendt, Ed and Kathy Rose, Randy and Michelle James, Rich and Lisa Griffis, Mark and Cassie Wallace, Ruth Roth, Mitzi Adams, Tara Lynn, Logan Carter, Jeff Eichorn, Jim Huk, Ryan and Mandy Miller, Pam and Jim Wallace, Mark and Shelley Mawhorter, the Zimmerman family and Don Detter. And, of course, E.J., Brad, Sherry, Trever and Keaton Sebring.

And thanks to all the former players for always allowing me – trusting me – to tell their stories. It's been an honor.

The information in this book is current as of October 2017. Some of these stories appeared previously in The News-Sentinel in Fort Wayne.

MORE BOOKS BY BLAKE SEBRING

Tales of the Komets

Legends of the Komets

Live from Radio Rinkside: The Bob Chase Story

The Biggest Mistake I Never Made (with Lloy Ball)

The Lake Effect

Homecoming Game

Fort Wayne Sports History

Lethal Ghost

Available at blakesebring.com

FOREWORD

Note: Don Detter started his 40th season as a statistician for the Komets in 2017-18.

It must have been early October 1952 when my Dad asked me if I knew anything about ice hockey. Being 8 years old – as probably with most people of Fort Wayne – I didn't know anything about ice hockey.

He told me that the new Allen County War Memorial Coliseum was finished, and that it was where the National Basketball Association's Fort Wayne Zollner Pistons and the new hockey team, the Komets, would be playing. He said the Komets would be having an exhibition to explain the rules and how the game was played.

Mom, Dad and I went and immediately got hooked.

The only sporting events I had attended before then were the world champion Zollner Pistons fast-pitch softball team at Municipal Beach diamond (later Zollner Stadium), the Daisies of the American Girls Professional Baseball League at Memorial Park and the Zollner Pistons basketball team at the North Side High School gym.

We went to a couple of Komets games each month for two years, and then got season tickets in 1954 and kept them until 1970. When attending the games, I would get a broken stick and a puck every once in a while and take them home. Dad would help me repair the stick, and I would go out in the street and knock the puck around. This caused the neighborhood kids to ask questions and want to play also. That started "hockey fever" in my neighborhood, and I am sure other kids did the same thing in their neighborhoods. Then you started seeing more kids playing hockey in the winter on the ponds at Franke, Lakeside and Reservoir parks. The only problem was there wasn't any place to buy proper hockey equipment until 1957 or 1958.

Just to give you an idea how primitive our hockey equipment was back then, we used adult-size figure skates. We would shove socks in the front of the skates and wear several pairs on our feet so the skates would fit better and we could skate. Hockey gloves were nonexistent. We would wear one pair of gloves and put a sock on top of our hand, then put a larger pair of work gloves over the glove and sock. Shin pads were either a baseball catcher's shin pads or newspapers that we had soaked in water and set outside overnight to freeze. We would tie the frozen newspapers to our legs, curving them to fit, when we skated at the park ponds. Every so often, we would have to stop playing as the papers started to thaw and we would take them off and let them refreeze. Goalies used baseball catchers' chest protectors or phone books. Sticks were usually repaired broken sticks from Komet games. There were no helmets, goalie masks or nets to shoot at, just piles of snow about 6 feet apart. This just shows you how much we loved the game.

In 1957, things changed in Fort Wayne as Ken Ullyot and Colin Lister were hired to manage the Komets. They had the experience and knowledge to manage and grow hockey in a community. They knew if they got the kids hooked on hockey, the parents would follow. It worked, and hockey became really big in Fort Wayne.

With the help of others, they formed youth hockey leagues at McMillen Park and had an artificial ice surface constructed over a tennis court. There were no walls or roof, just hockey in the open air. Komet players helped coach the teams, and good hockey equipment was starting to become available at several stores downtown.

The youth hockey programs had to have someone to run and supervise them, and those people were the real stars that no one knew about. They were there to keep order among chaos. They supervised the resurfacing of the ice, worked in the warming house, set game and practice schedules, and a million other things. Without those people, the youth hockey program would not have survived. Those people included Jim Ramage, Bob Arnold, Richard Zimmerman Sr., Flossie Zimmerman, Norm Foster, Mitzi Berg-Toepfer, Roy Chin and a bunch more that I cannot remember, for which I apologize.

Then there were Jerry Nuerge and Tom Stumpf, who organized the better older players into a team called the Junior Komets. In 1958 or '59, the team joined the Midwest Amateur Hockey League, which was comprised of teams from Indianapolis, Cincinnati and Louisville, Ky. That league lasted until 1975, give or take a year. Several of the players were able to secure college hockey scholarships.

When Komet players started showing up to coach the youth hockey games, you couldn't believe how much it meant to us kids. Our heroes coaching us! WOW! The Komet players were really great at helping us become better players, and I speak from personal experience. Because of our friendship with Ron Ullyot, son of Komets coach Ken Ullyot, neighborhood friends

Jack Coles, Gary Myers and I started skating and practicing with the Komets in 1958. What an experience that was, having the Komets players showing us how to do things the proper way, players such as Eddie Long, Bill Short, Orrin Gould, Len Thornson, Andy Voykin and Con Madigan. For example, a couple of the tougher players showed us how to protect ourselves in a fight and how to fight. They even showed us how they filed their fingernails to a point so the fingernails would penetrate the heavy wool sweaters of the day and get through to the opponent's skin, thus distracting him. Ron, Gary and Jack all received full hockey scholarships with major Division I colleges in 1964. I remember that in 1962, when I called five or six colleges to ask about scholarships for hockey, they all asked me, "Do they play hockey in Indiana?" Just look where Fort Wayne is in the eyes of the hockey world today.

As hockey continued to grow in Fort Wayne, more players wanted to play for the Komets because Ken Ullyot knew people in the National Hockey League and some players were given the opportunity to move up. That started the pipeline from Fort Wayne to the NHL. The first was John Ferguson, who was signed by Montreal after the 1959-60 season and went on to have a stellar career with the Canadiens. There have been many players since who have graduated from the Komets and played in the NHL.

The same could be said of coaches. Researching hockeyDB.com, I found there have been 366 head coaches in the NHL, and 14 have come through Fort Wayne. One was an assistant coach, Gerard Gallant, who went on to coach in the NHL. Four were former Komets players: John Anderson, Fred Creighton, John Ferguson and Dirk Graham. There were three

Courtesy of The News-Sentinel

coaches that played for the Komets and then coached the Komets before coaching in the NHL. They are Marc Bouleau, Al Sims and Bruce Boudreau. Boudreau has been named Coach of the Year in the NHL. The last two, John Torchetti and Dave Allison, coached but did not play for the Komets. Gallant, Torchetti and Boudreau are still coaching in the NHL.

Not only have players and coaches developed here, but several off-ice personnel such as trainers, equipment managers and ice technicians have as well before being employed by NHL teams. As of this writing, only one Fort Wayne native, Snider High School graduate Fred Knipscheer, has made it to the NHL. But there will be more in the future. There have been several Fort Wayne natives who have played minor pro hockey in North America and Europe. There have been 26 former Komets who have played in the Olympics. Steve Janaszak and Mark Wells played on the 1980 "Miracle on Ice" USA gold-medal team. Wally Schreiber won two silver medals for Canada in 1992 and 1994. Jim Burton, in my opinion the best defenseman ever to play for the Komets, played for Austria. Dan Ratushny also won a silver medal for Canada in 1992.

But to me, there have been two outstanding results of hockey fever in Fort Wayne. First has been the many former Komets that have decided to make Fort Wayne their permanent home. They have gotten excellent jobs and contributed much to the community. The second is the number of local and area hockey players who have obtained college scholarships. Both the retired Komets and local athletes have made it to the big leagues because of the lessons and values learned from the Komets organization, starting with Eddie Long, then to Ken Ullyot and Colin Lister, and now with the Franke Family. The success in life after hockey that so many have achieved can be traced, in great part, to the caliber of people brought to Fort Wayne and the values they passed on to the Fort Wayne youth.

I personally cannot thank the Komets organization enough for what they taught me about life and how to be a good citizen.

I hope you take the time to read this log of 65 years of the Komets' influence on the hockey world – from an idea on a napkin by a couple of enterprising promoters, to the Ullyot and Lister years with their hockey experience and knowledge, through a few tough years, and finally with the Franke family, to help grow this franchise into a bastion of strength and honesty in the hockey industry. The Komets took a small city in northeast Indiana where "do they play hockey in Indiana?" was said in the '50s and early '60s and turned it into the second-oldest minor league hockey franchise in the United States. How the Komets recruited so many quality hockey people to Fort Wayne and how they helped so many young people obtain college scholarships and grow into quality, productive adults is a great read. I hope you have as much fun reading this book by this author as I had talking and working with my friend, Blake Sebring. Enjoy.

Don Detter
Aug. 29, 2017

CHAPTER 1

Fergie left his mark on the game

John and Joan Ferguson
Courtesy of Ferguson family

John Ferguson came to the Komets in 1959 as a raw rookie left wing and quit playing in 1971 as one of hockey's greatest winners with five Stanley Cup rings.

Ferguson was the first member of the Fort Wayne Komets to make it to the National Hockey League as a player, which led to some interesting quotes in his book Thunder and Lightning.

"This may sound hard to believe, but the Fort Wayne Komets were the toughest team I ever had to make, throughout my entire career," Ferguson wrote. "They had a lot of veterans and very few spots for a rookie to crack the lineup."

Komets coach Ken Ullyot had wanted the forward ever since Ferguson played against Ullyot's Prince Albert team in the Western Hockey League with Melville in the mid-1950s. Ferguson would later be known as perhaps the NHL's toughest player ever, but he struggled mightily in the first half of the season in Fort Wayne, with only two goals by Christmas. He started playing much more physically in the second half and scored 30 goals as the Komets had their best regular season ever in 1959-60.

Ferguson spent only the one season in Fort Wayne, scoring 32 goals and 65 points with 126 penalty minutes. Then he moved to Cleveland of the American Hockey League for three seasons before joining the Montreal Canadiens in 1963 to protect Jean Beliveau. Ferguson fought the Bruins' Ted Green just 12 seconds into his first NHL game – winning the brawl and then scoring two goals and an assist in a 4-4 tie in Boston.

Ullyot always knew Ferguson would make it to the NHL.

"He was a very good student," Ullyot said. "He was strong, and he stood out with his ability. He just needed to work on a few things."

After giving Ullyot credit for turning him into an NHL player, Ferguson said in his post-career book that Ullyot was the best coach in hockey.

Though he was small by today's standards at 5 feet 11 inches and 190 pounds, Ferguson also was very tough, leading the NHL in fights twice early in his career.

"He never looked for a fight and never hit a guy dirty," Komets linemate Eddie Long said. "He played the game first, and then he fought. Everybody saw him fight once and then left him alone. He really worked at the game."

Ferguson used those skills for eight seasons to protect Montreal stars Beliveau and Bernie Geoffrion, earning almost 1,214 penalty minutes in his 500-game career with 67 career fights. He also scored 145 goals and 303 points. His highest penalty-minute total for a season was 185.

As Beliveau said, "The point is that Fergie wasn't, and didn't have to be, a nonstop brawler. His hard-earned reputation preceded him, and he could keep the opposition in line without spending all night in the penalty box."

He was so respected as a player that Ferguson led all rookies in scoring his first season and finished second for the Calder Cup Trophy to teammate Jacques Laperriere, a defenseman. During his best season, he scored 29 goals with a plus-30 rating in 1968-69, the same year he scored the Stanley Cup-clinching goal. Twice he played in the NHL All-Star Game, something unheard of for a player who was primarily thought of as an enforcer. He scored at last 15 goals in four of his first five seasons (with 30 game-winning goals) and earned at least 100 penalty minutes every season.

"I think Fergie was the toughest fighter I encountered in all my years in the NHL," former Canadiens coach Scotty Bowman said. "The Canadiens were a bit small, and they were more skillful than strong, but he came in and turned them around and they won five cups."

During Ferguson's eight-year NHL career, the Canadiens won Stanley Cups in 1965, 1966, 1968, 1969 and 1971. After clinching the 1971 title against Chicago in seven games, Ferguson shocked everyone in the Montreal locker room by announcing his immediate retirement at age 32. The Canadiens tried convincing him to return, but Ferguson held firm.

Ferguson started a very successful post-playing career by serving as an assistant coach with Team Canada in the 1972 Summit Series against the Soviets, considered by some as the best hockey series ever. Ferguson became the New York Rangers coach and general manager for two seasons and then general manager of the Winnipeg Jets. The Jets won the World Hockey Association's AVCO World Trophy in 1979 under Ferguson's direction. After finishing a 10-year run in Winnipeg, he later worked for the Ottawa Senators as a director of player personnel and was responsible for finding all-star Daniel Alfredsson.

Ferguson died at age 68 in 2007 following a long battle with prostate cancer. Even near the end of his life, he kept in touch with Ullyot and some of his old Fort Wayne teammates.

Major league teams that have lasted longer in the same city than the Komets

NFL

Chicago Bears, Detroit Lions,
Green Bay Packers, Philadelphia Eagles,
Pittsburgh Steelers, Washington Redskins

NBA

New York Knicks, Boston Celtics

NHL

Boston Bruins, Chicago Blackhawks,
Detroit Red Wings, Montreal Canadiens,
New York Rangers, Toronto Maple Leafs

MLB

New York Yankees, Boston Red Sox,
Chicago White Sox, Cleveland Indians,
Detroit Tigers, Chicago Cubs,
St. Louis Cardinals, Cincinnati Reds,
Philadelphia Phillies, Pittsburgh Pirates

CHAPTER 2

Adamson made big impression on Canadiens

It's partly because of the Montreal Canadiens that Chuck Adamson became the first Fort Wayne Komets goaltender to regularly wear a mask.

Adamson had just arrived in Fort Wayne in 1962 after playing three seasons for the Indianapolis Chiefs, and the 1962-63 International Hockey League season was only nine games old when the Canadiens came to Memorial Coliseum for an exhibition game on Nov. 20.

"It was just another game because it was right at the start of the season, but you were still trying to establish yourself," Adamson said. "I was certainly on trial."

He passed. Playing before 4,630 fans, Adamson made 62 saves. The score was 3-1 for most of the contest after the Komets' Len Thornson put in a rebound of an Eddie Long shot, but the Canadiens won 4-1.

"Chuck single-handedly kept us in that game," former Komets business manager and owner Colin Lister recalled.

Afterward, Montreal coach Toe Blake said, "If your goalie plays like that all the time, we'll take him back with us."

Luckily for the Komets, Blake was only joking. Adamson went on to have an outstanding season and lead the Komets to their first Turner Cup championship.

“I think that game helped us build our confidence,” Long said.

Most of the Komets were familiar with the Canadiens, having tried out with the team in previous years. Adamson had been part of Montreal training camps as a youngster. In fact, he lived near relatives of Blake in Falconbridge, Ont.

“The funny thing is, I think there were probably six or seven guys on that team who I had played junior against,” Adamson said. “Montreal took me to training camp when I was 18, and I played about eight exhibition games with Henri Richard. I was nervous about this game, but not really, because in junior I had played four games against Montreal.”

Thornson also had regularly attended Montreal training camps before settling in Fort Wayne.

“For us to play a big team like that was fabulous,” Thornson said. “I knew quite a few of them. Deep in your mind you want to really look good because everyone has major league aspirations. The second thought to go through your head is, ‘God, I don’t want to be blown out by these guys.’”

The Canadiens had stars such as Richard, Jacques Plante, Boom Boom Geoffrion and Jean Beliveau.

“We weren’t awed by them, and that’s why we played a good game,” Long said. “Charlie was the difference, because it could have been 15-1.”

During the third period, Adamson was struck in the face on a shot by Richard. The game was stopped while Adamson was

Montreal Canadiens John Ferguson, Bernie Geoffrion and Jean Beliveau greet Komets Eddie Long, Lionel Repka and Len Thornson before a 1963 exhibition game.
Courtesy of The News-Sentinel

getting stitches, so Richard and Geoffrion put on a show while Jack Loos played the organ.

"As they skated down the ice, they passed the puck to each other without it touching the ice," recalls current Komets owner Stephen Franke, who was 13 at the time. "I remember it very vividly in my mind. I remember the crowd was sitting on their hands because they didn't know if we would get creamed."

Montreal played the game with 11 forwards and 18 players, and the Komets played with seven forwards, five defensemen and one goaltender.

"They got $100 for playing the game, and we got a handshake and a Pepsi," Thornson joked.

After the game, Plante asked Adamson why he didn't wear a mask.

Plante had become the first NHL goaltender to regularly wear a mask during a game on Nov. 1, 1959, when a backhand from the New York Rangers' Andy Bathgate caught Plante in the upper lip. After a trip to the dressing room for stitches, Plante returned, saying he would not play unless he could wear his goalie mask. Because the teams had only one goaltender at the time, Montreal coach Blake had no option but to agree. The Canadiens won 3-1, and the next game, Plante again wore the mask despite Blake's objections. It didn't hurt that the Canadiens then went 18 games without a loss with Plante wearing the mask.

So Adamson took Plante's advice and, after wearing a mask in practice for a while, wore one in a game for the first time on Dec. 22, 1962, as the Komets beat St. Paul 2-1.

"It's a little uncomfortable because I sweat so much, but I think it'll work out all right," he told The News-Sentinel's Bud Gallmeier after the game. "I have trouble seeing the puck at my feet, but then every mask gives you that blind spot."

Up to that point in his career, Adamson estimated he'd been hit in the face 11 times for more than 200 stitches. Today, Adamson figures the mask saved his eyesight and saved his face about another 100 stitches. Wearing the original white mask, which cost $35, he led the Komets to their first Turner Cup championship in 1963. He used another mask that he bought from Plante for $150 to help the Komets win the 1965 Turner Cup.

He also was wearing a mask the next time the Canadiens returned on Nov. 26, 1963, and made 44 saves, but the Komets lost 7-1 as the Canadiens obviously wanted to teach the Komets a lesson.

"They really didn't give us much of a chance," Adamson said. "They jumped on us right away."

There was an added attraction during that game – former Komet John Ferguson was in his rookie season with Montreal playing on a line with Beliveau and Geoffrion. The Komets owners thought that would help increase the crowd, but only 2,422 fans showed up.

Detroit Red Wings great Gordie Howe meets Pierre Brilliant of Indianapolis and Eddie Long of Fort Wayne at the 1958 IHL All-Star Game.

Courtesy of The News-Sentinel

NHL teams in Fort Wayne

Feb. 17, 1957 • Detroit 11, IHL All-Stars 3
Attendance: 3,900

Nov. 20, 1962 • Montreal 4, Komets 1
Attendance: 4,630

Nov. 26, 1963 • Montreal 7, Komets 1
Attendance: 2,422

Oct. 4, 1974 • Detroit 3, Indianapolis (WHA) 3
Attendance: 3,523

Komets vs. Russian teams

Dec. 31, 1975 • Spartak 7, Komets 4
Attendance: 6,030

Dec. 7, 1989 • Komets 0, Sokol Kiev 0
Attendance: 1,907

Feb. 20, 1994 • Komets 6, Russian Penguins 1
Attendance: 8,103

Nov. 5, 1994 • Komets 5, Soviet Wings 2
Attendance: 7,044

CHAPTER 3

A memorable souvenir

Billy Richardson
Courtesy of The News-Sentinel

About a year before he died on Dec. 5, 2011, at age 85, former Komet Billy Richardson showed his daughter something special, something she didn't know had been hidden under her parents' bed for almost 50 years.

By Nov. 20, 1962, Richardson had retired as a player but continued in hockey as a linesman. His story really starts a few months before that when Montreal Canadiens coach Toe Blake called Memorial Coliseum General Manager Don Myers trying to set up an exhibition hockey game. Myers walked down to the Komets' office to give Fort Wayne coach Ken Ullyot the message.

The Canadiens, who had already won 12 Stanley Cups including five straight from 1956 to 1960, were scheduled to play in Chicago on Nov. 18 and in Detroit on Nov. 22 for Thanksgiving. Rather than go home and face the hassle of the border crossing, Blake wanted to stop in Fort Wayne. Ullyot was agreeable and picked former Komet Hartley McLeod to referee the game, assisted by linesmen Gus Braumberger and Richardson.

Featuring a lineup of six future Hall of Fame players, the Canadiens won the match 4-1, outshooting the Komets 66-24 despite a Herculean performance by Fort Wayne goaltender

Chuck Adamson. The crowd was 4,630, which was excellent for a Tuesday night.

After the game, Richardson asked Canadiens star Jean Beliveau for his stick, and Beliveau convinced his teammates to sign it. The names include Hall of Fame members Tom Johnson, Bernie "Boom Boom" Geoffrion, Henri Richard, Dickie Moore and Jacques Plante, along with retired University of Michigan coach Red Berenson, who will likely be inducted eventually.

There's a reason the Canadiens were billed as "The World's Greatest Hockey Team" even though they would be knocked out of the playoffs in the first round the next two years. They won in 1965 and 1966, lost in the 1967 finals, and then won again in 1968 and 1969, led by former Komet John Ferguson.

In 2012, Richardson's daughter, Janet Richardson-Megles, decided to put the stick up for auction, and a fan purchased it.

Because the stick was kept away from light under the bed, it was preserved in excellent condition and only the signature of center Don Marshall had faded.

"He never talked about it. It was just under the bed," Richardson-Megles said. "He said, 'I wish I knew what we could do with it, because it might be worth something.' He just said make sure you don't let anybody have it."

Most of the Komets players were only sorry they had not thought of asking for a Montreal stick.

"I knew Billy had that stick because he told me about it," former Komets great Len Thornson said. "In those days, you could go in the dressing room between periods. They might have put him in there because it was an exhibition game, and it didn't mean much to those guys."

CHAPTER 4

Komets game sent Emrick's life in new direction

As he was growing up, Mike Emrick dreamed of becoming a baseball announcer until Dec. 10, 1960, when he attended his first hockey game, the Komets vs. the Muskegon Zephyrs. Emrick, then 14, and his brother Dan had watched hockey on TV through snowy reception because their home in LaFontaine, Ind. (located about an hour south of Fort Wayne), wasn't close enough to Indianapolis or Fort Wayne. They also listened to announcer Bob Chase describe Komets games on WOWO, with Emrick jiggling the radio dial to give the signal a little extra strength.

After frequently bugging their parents to drive from LaFontaine to see a Komets game at Memorial Coliseum, the boys got their wish.

Charles, Emrick's father, was a high school principal who also owned a music store.

"He decided he would make it a store party, and all the piano teachers and the other employees would meet us at Colonel Sanders Hobby Ranch House (in Fort Wayne)," Mike Emrick recalled. "We had a grand table, and then we went to the hockey game. He footed the bill for 25, 30 people. We were just glad to be inside and see a game."

Emrick had never seen anything as white as the ice or as blue as the Muskegon uniforms, he remembered.

"You are forming wonderful opinions, and everything is fantastic," he said. "There's nothing jaded about anything at all. It was one of those fantastic nights."

A year after setting their all-time record for points and wins in a season, the Komets had lost four games in a row heading into the Muskegon game. The Zephyrs led 3-1 with 10 minutes left when Len Thornson scored to give the Komets a chance. Then Con Madigan tied it with 17 seconds remaining, skating backward around the rink to celebrate.

Neither team scored in overtime, but Emrick's highlight was watching Madigan fight Zephyrs player-coach Moose Lallo with two seconds left. There was also organist Norm Carroll playing "Santa Claus is Coming to Town." Another favorite memory was watching Chase standing in the press box to lean over the WOWO banner and call the play.

"I still enjoy baseball as much as a Pirates fan can, but once that night happened, I became a hockey fanatic," Emrick said.

Whenever possible, Emrick and his friends would drive up to be part of the Saturday night crowds. Eventually, he started taking along a tape recorder, sitting in the upper-deck corners to practice calling a game. Then a couple days later, he'd take the tape to Chase at WOWO, and they would talk about it.

"I gave him a few little hints and stuff to get started, but holy cow, you could already tell he had so much enthusiasm for what he was doing," Chase said in his biography. "This just kept rolling, and he got better and better at it."

After graduating from Southwood High School, Emrick attended Manchester College and continued to attend Komets games, building an even closer relationship with Chase. While Emrick was working on his master's degree at Miami (Ohio) in 1969, Komets business manager Colin Lister arranged for Emrick to receive a Commissioner's Pass, which allowed him to get into any International Hockey League game for free.

Emrick kept sending out applications and audition tapes to every minor league hockey team, finally finding a job for the 1973-74 season with Port Huron.

"For $160 a week, I was in hog heaven," Emrick said. "I had finally arrived."

Mike Emrick and Bob Chase

Courtesy of The News-Sentinel

Actually, he was just getting started – and is now the best hockey broadcaster in the world, maybe the best announcer in any sport. During his 40-plus-year career, he has called 37 NHL seasons, 18 Stanley Cup Finals and seven Olympics on his way to the Hockey Hall of Fame.

"Ernie (Harwell) would always say, 'A man is very lucky if God gives him a job to do that he enjoys.' I always give that quote when I get an award. That's it. You realize when you get to see a hockey game and you get in free, that's No. 1, and you get a good seat. You get to see the best players, and twice a month you get something in the mail."

It all started Dec. 10, 1960, in Fort Wayne.

CHAPTER 5

Radio call was a perfect memory

About a minute after signing off his post-game show Nov. 9, 2012, Komets announcer Bob Chase's daughter Karin called from Colorado.

"Dad, Vic and I were going out to eat, but we couldn't leave until it was over because you guys were having so much fun," she said. "Was that ever something!"

"I got her approval," Chase said with a more energetic grin than an 86-year-old should have at 11 p.m. after a long day.

Anyone who listened to Fort Wayne's 5-2 win over Evansville that night approved as Chase shared the booth with regular color man Robbie Irons and America's voice of hockey, Mike Emrick from NBC. Though Chase had been defining hockey radio broadcasts for 60 years and Emrick on the television side for 40, this was the first time they described a game together.

When the LaFontaine-native Emrick started his career as a teenager, he'd sit in a Memorial Coliseum corner talking into a tape recorder. A few years later, he shared some of his recordings with Chase at WOWO, and that relationship grew into a gift for the sport they love. Emrick took Chase's passion and dedication to the world's stage and then refined it to his own level of grace and precision.

No mentor could be more approving, no student more respectful.

Mike Emrick and Bob Chase
Courtesy of The News-Sentinel

Considering that by this night they had probably collectively broadcast more than 8,000 pro hockey games, it's something of a miracle that Chase and Emrick had never called a game together. After all, they've possibly talked more hockey than any two men in history, and when they aren't on the air, they are talking about it a lot with each other during regular phone calls. This time it worked out because the NHL was involved in a lockout, and it was a way to celebrate Chase's 60th season with the Komets.

"It's sort of like 'Field of Dreams,' though not with father and son," Emrick said the day before the game. "It's more of an icon and the guy who grew up listening to him. We have to be careful to translate that fun so the audience enjoys it, too."

Putting them together for one game, they exceeded even a perfectionist's expectations. With Irons, the trio had fun calling the game, and that helped make sure everyone listening did, too – even a good part of the 7,707 Memorial Coliseum fans who had earphones plugged into radios or smartphones.

"Sometimes , when you have the idea, 'We're just going to have fun,' ... something happens and you all of a sudden forget that," Emrick said. "Fortunately, I don't think that happened tonight. We're pleased if people had a good time."

How could they help it? That was guaranteed by the preparation Emrick and Chase had put in for two and a half hours at the morning skate. As Emrick quizzed every stick boy and player, they all looked like they were 10 years old and meeting Santa Claus.

"It was a big thrill for a lot of guys," Komets coach Al Sims said. "Even some of the guys from the American League had to come to Fort Wayne to meet Mike Emrick. It was a pretty neat thing."

And though forgetting about the broadcasters as soon as the opening faceoff fell to the ice, the Komets were maybe a little more determined to win than usual. It was the only time they would ever have the world's best announcer call a game they were playing in, after all. Emrick had called the Olympics, National Hockey League All-Star Games, World Cups, Stanley Cup Finals and now a Komets game. To the players, this time the broadcaster added to the prestige of the event and raised their level.

"Any time Mike Emrick is broadcasting your game, you want to make a good impression," forward Kaleigh Schrock said. "He knew more about me than I knew about myself. To have him with Chaser, that was a real honor to play in that game."

The broadcast itself wasn't perfect. It was better than that. Squeezing into the small home radio booth that was built for two people, the trio eventually forgot they were trying to fit in and around each other and just called the game. Without realizing it, they did what they do better than anyone. The laughs flowed with the game.

At one point, Emrick remarked that it had been at least 10 years since he'd called a game on radio, which is much different than describing the action on television.

"You have a lot of right-wing boards and left boards and near corner and far corner that you don't say on television," he said. "If you get paid by the word, and I hope Bob does, you earn double the money in radio."

There also were some classic Emrick calls. Any rust from the NHL lockout was scraped away like a goaltender scratching up his crease before the national anthem or a first-period facewash in the corner.

"Some discouraging words there from Henley in the face of Aaron Gens."

A late second-period post-whistle group shoving match was described, "A little extra from Rizk, and a crowd will gather at the horn!"

Adding Emrick's descriptions to Chase's enthusiasm and Irons' explanations was about as perfect as a minor league game could hope to be called. The less they tried, the better the game became to anyone listening.

"It's another highlight for the year 2012," said Chase, who had recently received the Lester Patrick Award for service to hockey in the United States. "I don't know what goes on next. Like I said in my wrap, in my fondest dreams, I never realized this could happen. I never even dreamt of it happening until now."

Best of all? It sounded like a dream, too, one that every listener will always remember.

CHAPTER 6

Madigan became the NHL's oldest rookie

Just before Christmas 1972, Con Madigan received a phone call from St. Louis Blues General Manager Lynn Patrick, who was looking for someone to take over his Denver farm team as player-coach. The Blues had just bought out Madigan's contract with Portland of the Western Hockey League, and Patrick was sure Madigan would be thrilled with the new assignment.

"I said no," Madigan said. "That's not what I wanted. I told him, 'I hear you guys have a couple of defensemen hurt, and I can play in St. Louis.'"

A lifelong minor leaguer, Madigan was an enforcing defenseman who could actually play offensively as well, earning all-league honors eight times, including a then-record 272 penalty minutes along with 57 points for the 1959-60 Komets. He was tough enough that few challenged him unless they were trying to make a name for themselves, and he finished his career with 18 consecutive seasons of at least 100 penalty minutes.

Following the 1967-68 expansion from the original six to 12 teams, Madigan already should have been playing in the NHL, but Portland would not release his rights. This was, finally at age 38, his chance at the show.

Instead of being offended with Madigan's brashness, Patrick told him to get on a plane and come in for a tryout. But, Patrick said, if Madigan didn't make the team he'd have to go to Denver.

"I was there for five days, and (Blues star) Garry Unger came up and told me they were signing me," Madigan said.

Con Madigan
Courtesy of Fort Wayne Komets

And that's how Madigan set a remarkable record on Feb. 1, 1973, becoming the oldest rookie in NHL history by playing in a game at Montreal. Madigan played 20 games that season and five more in the playoffs, mostly pairing with Blues all-star Bob Plager, finishing with three assists and 25 penalty minutes. Though he was officially a rookie, Madigan was easily the oldest player on the team, just a few months older than defenseman Bob McCord and two years younger than coach Jean-Guy Talbot.

"I had a lot of fun," said Madigan, who continues to live in Portland, Ore. "Guys were really good to me. All I did was pass the puck a little quicker. It was just as easy to play in the NHL as it was in the Western League, the guys were just younger. There were a lot of players in the WHL who could have played in the NHL, but there was no way to do it! They owned you, and you had to do what they said."

Madigan even fought a few times that season, especially in Philadelphia, home of the Broad Street Bullies.

"There were a couple of guys in Philly, and I said, 'It's your building and you put the show on, but don't worry, when I hit you, you'll know it,'" Madigan recalled. He wasn't called "Mad Dog" for nothing!

Knowing they had younger players coming up over the following summer, the Blues gave Madigan the choice of going to Portland or San Diego, or to Denver as coach. He chose San Diego, with the parting gift of the last season of a two-year contract. About 40 games into the season, the Gulls' goaltender got hurt, and Madigan was traded back to Portland for a replacement.

"He was one of the toughest guys and characters in his day," former Canadiens coach Scotty Bowman said. "He was in an era where each team had a few fighters, but geeze, he was a tough guy, though."

By the time Madigan retired at age 40 in 1976, he'd earned 3,537 penalty minutes, which at the time were the second most in minor league hockey history. He was renowned enough to star as Ross "Mad Dog" Madison in the 1977 movie "Slap Shot".

Madigan retired in Portland where he worked as a pipefitter. The Buckaroos honored him with "Con Madigan Day" in 2009.

Spurred by the influx of veteran players from Eastern Europe, in 1990 the NHL changed its rookie classification rule. Now players are not considered rookies if they have passed their 26th birthday, meaning Madigan's record can never be broken.

CHAPTER 7

Komets received parts in "Slap Shot" movie

After its premiere in 1977, "Slap Shot" became the most-watched hockey movie of all time. Despite and sometimes because of the raunchy language, it's definitely the most quoted. Any hockey player from almost any age can quote parts of the movie, which has become a timeless staple on road trips.

The movie premiered nationally March 25, 1977, but it didn't arrive in Fort Wayne until April 18. The Komets had a hand in the movie, or three hands, actually. Former Komet Con Madigan and future Komets Bruce Boudreau and Jeff Carlson acted in the movie. Carlson, who played 14 games with the Komets toward the end of the 1980-81 season, was one of the legendary Hanson brothers.

The movie was filmed during the 1975-76 season in Johnstown, Pa., where Boudreau was playing for the North American Hockey League's Johnstown Jets.

"We'd play a game, and the next day we wouldn't practice because we'd be 10 hours on the set waiting to just get a couple of shots," Boudreau said. "As far as my part goes, I just tried to find a camera and stand in front of it all day long. I knew I wasn't going to get a chance at too many major motion pictures, so I was going to make the best of it."

Boudreau shows up in the movie twice, playing against Paul Newman's "Charlestown Chiefs." There's a long game sequence five minutes into the movie and another about an hour into the film. Boudreau is wearing jersey No. 7 and, of course, scores most of the goals for the "Hyannis Port Presidents."

"It was just like the regular season," joked Boudreau, one of minor league hockey's all-time-greatest scorers.

Boudreau said he taught Newman how to take a slap shot, and Newman's apartment in the movie is actually Boudreau's place, picked because it was the most dingy of all the players' apartments. Boudreau said he was paid $1,300 for two weeks of work.

Madigan plays Ross "Mad Dog" Madison of the "Syracuse Bulldogs," who never travels anywhere without his longtime friend and attorney, Sam "Small Print" Lyman. As he is introduced before the championship game at the end of the movie, Madison skates out telling the crowd they are No. 1 – but he isn't using his index finger.

"They had another deal and they wanted me to swear, but I said I have two girls and I don't think I want to do that," Madigan said. "I don't mind coming out and flipping the crowd off. I used to give them a kiss goodbye sometimes."

Madigan held the Komets' single-season record for penalty minutes in a season for nearly 20 years, setting the original mark of 272 in 1959-60. He played three seasons for the Komets and then bounced around the minors before settling in with Portland of the Western Hockey League. He retired in 1976 as the WHL's all-time-best defenseman.

A notorious minor league brawler, Madigan – whose actual nickname was "Mad Dog" – once was suspended for the rest of the season and fined $500 for knocking out a referee in 1971.

Madigan also had a part in how the whole "Slap Shot" film got started. One year in training camp with Portland, Madigan met a young player named Ned Dowd. A few years later when Madigan was playing with St. Louis in 1972 as the NHL's oldest-ever rookie at age 38, Dowd contacted him to ask for tickets to a playoff game for himself and his sister.

Bruce Boudreau

Courtesy of Minnesota Wild

A few years later, Nancy Dowd wrote "Slap Shot" based on the minor league adventures of her brother, who plays Ogie Ogilthorpe in the movie. Nancy remembered Madigan and called him in Portland to invite him to join the film.

"One of the neat things I remember was Paul Newman and his wife Joanne Woodward," Madigan said. "There must have been 700 guys there, and she remembered everybody's name. He'd take three guys to dinner every night, and we just sat there and told stories."

There were plenty of stories made during filming, too.

"We had a brawl one day," Madigan said. "Somebody hit somebody, and all of a sudden, people start pushing and we had a brawl going. They left it in the movie. That was the greatest thing, but they didn't want to pay any money."

Because he had a job back home and the filming lasted much longer than expected, Madigan eventually took his skates and sneaked away.

The film eventually made $28 million at the box office.

CHAPTER 8

Thomas served as the Hockey Guru one summer

About once a season during a road trip, Leo Thomas is going to hear abuse from his teammates 10 times worse than he will from any opposing fans.

That's just because they're all jealous, he'll say with a smile.

On most teams, the trainer controls the DVD selection on bus trips, and sometimes they'll include "The Love Guru" for one of the longer rides. The film was voted the Golden Raspberry as the worst movie of 2008, but Thomas says he had a blast working as an extra in the hockey scenes.

Rated PG-13 for a lot of raunchy language, the movie stars Mike Myers as the love guru who is trying to fix the love life of Toronto Maple Leafs star Darren Roanoke, played by Romany Malco. Thomas serves as Malco's double in the hockey scenes.

"We have a pro tournament in Toronto every summer, and at the last tournament, there was a guy looking for guys to be in the movie," Thomas said.

"It just turned out the lead guy was a black hockey player, and he saw me warming up and said, 'You should come out tomorrow morning.' There were probably seven guys going for the part, and I knew all of them."

Thomas was one of three selected as doubles for Malco. He

took care of the skating, stick-handling and scoring while the other two were used for stunt doubles.

"When you watch the movie, you can tell the difference," Thomas said. "You can tell how the guy is skating which guy is playing the part."

Thomas dominates the hockey scenes, succeeding with several moves and trick shots that would likely get him killed during a regular game.

The movie was filmed during the late summer of 2007, and Thomas missed the first four games of the season with Bloomington of the IHL. He said he made more money in a month and a half of filming than he did that entire season.

"I felt like I was dreaming every day I was filming that movie, hanging out with movie stars," he said. "It was something I couldn't give up. It was a once-in-a-lifetime thing I had to do."

Former Komet Travis Whitehead was heading into his junior season at Buffalo State when he was invited to the tryout for the movie, and he invited three of his teammates to go along. He served as an extra and appears in the background of several scenes.

Thomas had to report each day by 6 a.m. to makeup at Toronto's Air Canada Centre, and filming sometimes lasted until 1 a.m. Often the players sat around all day in the Maple Leafs' dressing room waiting. Sometimes it took 10 hours to shoot one shot in the movie, Thomas said.

"Certain days we'd say we are working on these three plays, but something would happen and it would take us about 10 hours," Thomas said. "Switching the cameras around would take two hours. I sat in the locker room once for 14 hours, playing cards and wearing half of my gear. It was exactly like a hockey team, which is why the actors loved it. They got a little taste of how we are in the dressing room and all the jokes that we have."

The payoff, Thomas said was getting his Maple Leafs jersey signed by everyone and attending the Toronto premiere. Even the extra grief he knew he'd take from his teammates was worth it.

"Some guys say it was a pretty bad movie, but they know it would have been an amazing experience," Thomas said.

Leo Thomas

Courtesy of The News-Sentinel

CHAPTER 9

"Miracle" gave former Komets greater appreciation for Brooks

Mark Wells climbed into his shower the night of Feb. 3, 2004, needing to talk with Herb Brooks, the legendary hockey coach who died Aug. 11, 2003, in an automobile accident.

The night before, Wells had attended the Hollywood premiere of "Miracle," the story of the 1980 United States Olympic hockey team, which was pushed by Brooks to a stunning upset of the Russians and, eventually, the gold medal.

"My spiritual belief is that he's only a blink away," the former Komets center said. "Now I can go on with life. 'Thank God for this movie, Herb, because I finally understand what you did.' There were some tears there."

The movie premiered Feb. 6, 2004, almost 24 years after the stunning upset.

Wells and former Komets goaltender Steve Janaszak were members of that team, and in particular, Brooks continually manipulated Wells. Several times, Wells was shipped out to minor league teams before being recalled the week before the Olympics. Wells was the last man named to the team that created history.

Though he scored two goals and played a vital defensive role in the Olympics, Wells tried for 24 years to make sense of Brooks and his Olympic experience. After seeing the movie, he finally found some peace with Brooks.

"The movie was so accurate that it made me feel like I got a monkey off my back," Wells said. "I understand him more so now than I ever did, even though I talked to him for years. Once you see the movie, you'll understand where I come from and what we went through as players. He tried to push us to a level beyond what we knew, and the results show what happened."

Wells, 46 when the movie came out, played 19 games for the Komets during the 1981-82 season, which turned out to be his last as a player. The experience with the Olympic team had stolen his fire for the game. At the time, he was recovering from three major back surgeries and finishing up his college work at Walsh College.

Janaszak, then 47, had a similar experience with the movie. A goaltender with the Komets during the 1980-81 season, he was 9-5-1 in pre-Olympic play but sat the bench in Lake Placid behind Jim Craig. He's now an investment banker living in Babylon, N.Y.

"I know the ending, we all know the ending, but even more than that I know the process," Janaszak said. "I lived through how that was all put together, and they take this story and in two hours pull all those emotions out of me."

Kurt Russell stars as Brooks and is the main focus of the story. Janaszak said Russell was so good in his portrayal it was almost like he was channeling Brooks, whom Janaszak also played for at the University of Minnesota.

The worst thing about sports movies usually is the sports scenes because they rarely come close to reality. But both Wells and Janaszak said "Miracle" comes pretty close.

“With the actual hockey footage, you could think you were watching a real game,” Janaszak said. “It’s all the way down to when Mike (Eruzione) scores the game-winning goal against the Russians, and there are still 10 minutes left in the game. It’s less time in the film, but it’s phenomenal how they put that together. You get concerned that this thing could come apart at any time.”

“You are going to find that this movie is not totally a sports movie,” Wells said. “It’s far beyond that. I think in the end you are going to understand Herb’s point. For me, this puts closure on who was this guy and why did he do it this way.

“I got goose bumps watching it, and some tears, too. This brought the whole crowd of Hollywood people to their feet, chanting ‘USA! USA!’ and that’s hard to do.”

CHAPTER 10

Janaszak helped behind the scenes during Olympics

For the first time since they shocked the world by winning the 1980 Olympic hockey gold medal, the living players from the "Miracle on Ice" United States team gathered Feb. 20, 2015, in Lake Placid, N.Y., to celebrate their 35th anniversary. That meant former Komet Steve Janaszak drove up from his home in Babylon, N.Y., and former Komet Mark Wells flew in from Harrison Township, Mich.

"The only time we had all 20 guys together was at an NHL All-Star Game right before the (2002) Salt Lake City Olympics," Janaszak said. "It was actually a lot of fun. There were a lot of the same jokes."

Some of the players have dealt with tough times since 1980, but Janaszak's toughest adversity came during the Olympics. After playing 17 pre-Olympic games, the goaltender never got off the bench during the tournament as Jim Craig started.

"Sitting the bench was probably the hardest thing I ever did," he said. "We're all wired to play. That's what you are there for, and you sit there and keep your mouth shut. It was a little bit of a different challenge."

To keep busy, Janaszak did whatever he could to help out, including sharpening all the players' skates. When he was a teenager, he worked for a small St. Paul, Minn., company that hand-made skate blades. He could sharpen 300, 400 at a time.

"That was my contribution," he said. "I could do it better than our equipment guy. I could do that with my eyes closed."

Janaszak jokes that he had the best seat in the house to watch history, but also that he was the luckiest guy on the team. He also met his future wife, Jaclyn, who was working as an interpreter for the International Olympic Committee.

After the Olympics, the Colorado Rockies prospect bounced from the American Hockey League with Baltimore to the Central Hockey League with Fort Worth and Wichita. Then Janaszak was sent to the Komets for the 1980-81 season, where he remembers that coach Moose Lallo was a character and that he split goaltending duties with Robbie Irons.

Steve Janaszak

"(Irons) is a very, very talented guy, and I learned a lot from him that year," Janaszak said. "He was there every night, that's what I remember the most. He showed me what it takes to be there to show up and work hard every night even though sometimes it's a grind."

After playing 42 games and giving up a 3.55 goals-against average with the Komets, Janaszak was named the International Hockey League's top American-born rookie. The next year, he went back to Fort Worth and later played again for the United States in the World Championships. He was bought out of his contract after the 1982-83 season and retired.

Ever since, he has run his investment management business in New York and helped Jaclyn raise their two daughters. He keeps a low profile around home, saying there are neighbors who probably don't even realize he was a hockey player.

Nostalgia about the 1980 team peaked in 2004 when the movie "Miracle" came out. Even then, he had an even-keeled perspective. While Janaszak was speaking at a grade school, one little girl, about 8, told him she liked the movie, but her favorite sports movie was "Seabiscuit." Janaszak laughed.

"One thing that time distorts is all the memories," he said. "They tend to really minimize the bad things, and all the good stuff is kind of like a fish story – it gets bigger and bigger every time you tell it.

"It has a life unto itself. A lot of people are still very touched by the story, and it doesn't get old. Whenever you are talking to somebody about it, I think it was Dave Christian who said it, the story always ends with a smile on everybody's face. How can that ever get old?"

CHAPTER 11

Wells holds hope despite health problems

How desperate would someone need to be to sell his or her Olympic gold medal, something they had sacrificed everything for, even the chance to make a fortune as a professional? What could happen to crush hope that much?

For many of his teammates on the 1980 United States Olympic hockey team, Mark Wells, 59 in 2017, is the player who disappeared. He stopped playing in 1981 after 19 games with the Fort Wayne Komets and went home to St. Clair Shores, Mich., figuring he'd already seen the ultimate in his hockey career and wondering whether the same was true of his life.

After he had made the team at Bowling Green State as a walk-on and then survived the cuts to make the national team, Wells was continually manipulated by coach Herb Brooks before the Olympics. He was used as the example for the rest of the team, several times getting shipped out to minor league teams. He even overcame a broken ankle before being recalled the week before the Olympics, the last man named to the team that made history.

Though the center had scored a ridiculous 232 points in 154 college games, Wells was asked by Brooks to concentrate on defense. Wells scored two goals and played a vital fourth-line role in the Olympics, probably playing more minutes than anyone against the Russians.

"My mission was to shut down the other team's top line, and I did my job," Wells said. "I was like the shadow, and I shut down everybody. I was the only guy walking around the Olympic Village telling everyone we were going to win. Everybody said, 'But you just lost to the Russians 10-3!' But I hadn't played that game."

And then he laughed.

During the tournament, he backed up his confidence. Opponents never scored a goal while he was on the ice, and at the end, he proved his worth and celebrated with his teammates. After a trip to the White House and a quick celebration back home, Wells played the next year with New Haven of the American Hockey League before bouncing around Oklahoma City, Flint and finally Fort Wayne.

Mark Wells

Courtesy of Detroit Free Press

"Montreal had traded my rights after the Olympics, and I was disheartened and lost my enthusiasm and drive," Wells said. "I had always dreamed of playing with the Canadiens. I'd had a great hockey career and had experienced one of the greatest moments of all time."

He went home to help a buddy run a restaurant but wrenched his back while moving some produce. After not missing a day of work in five years, Wells had to be carried out of the restaurant and faced immediate surgery. Though doctors didn't realize it at the time, he had a genetic spinal degenerative disc disorder. The first surgery lasted 12 hours, and afterward doctors told him the damage was more extensive than expected.

He spent three years bedridden inside a body cast hoping the vertebrae would fuse, but then another surgery revealed the screws had broken off. That meant three more years in a body cast. This time, doctors prescribed heroin for the pain, but eventually even that failed, so Wells tried OxyContin and nerve blocks.

"I started to feel extreme pain to the point of suicide," he said. "My spirits kept falling, and I said, 'My life is over. I'll never have a wife or kids.' I was in so much pain that nothing mattered to me. I had no idea how to survive or exist."

Wells spent nine years in a body cast, was declared disabled and, in 2002, sold his medal for $40,000 to help pay the bills. It later sold at an auction for more than $300,000.

How did he survive? He says he couldn't rely on anything but faith.

"I have an athlete's mentality of toughness and hope, and that helped me to be a powerful, spiritual person to fight this disease," he said. "I have God all over my room, and Mother Mary. I read about the Spirit that said, 'I will see you one day, my son, in a better place.' I pray every day to make a little bit of progress."

Though Wells also suffered a stroke in March 2013, he recovered and faces more surgery. Still, some positive things are finally happening. Wells and his partner, Tonia Flenna, have had two boys. St. Clair Shores, Mich., renamed the municipal rink in his honor in 2014. He also took part in a 2015 35-year reunion with his Olympic teammates.

"This thing grew beyond anything we ever dreamed of, and it will be here for 285 years, not just 35," he said. "None of us realized the importance this would have on society still today."

After the reunion, he underwent another back surgery, his sixth. Recovering took a year, and Wells slept in a lift chair for three months. Three months? That's nothing, he said.

"I have high hopes and very big plans," he said. "After the dedication of the rink... it (gave) me an opportunity, a hope of inspiring all the youth players in St. Clair Shores. They are witnessing a man who has done it, and my focus is on those youth now. It gives me hope to build a larger foundation."

Finally, Mark Wells has a flicker of hope again.

Komets who played in the Olympics

2006 Konstantin Shafranov, Kazakhstan • **2002** Igor Bondarev, Latvia; Konstantin Simchuk, Andrei Srubko and Igor Chibirev, Ukraine; Len Soccio, Germany; Vladimir Tsyplakov, Oleg Mikulchik, Andrei Mezin and Sergei Stas, Belarus • **1998** Shafranov, Kazakhstan; Tsyplakov and Stas, Belarus • **1994** Wally Schreiber, Canada; Jim Burton and Rob Doyle, Austria; Oleg Shargorodsky, Russia • **1992** Viacheslav Butsayev, Unified Team; David Tretowicz and Ray LeBlanc, United States; Dan Ratushny and Schreiber, Canada • **1988** John Blue, United States; Schreiber, Todd Strueby, Serge Roy, Chris Felix and Bob Joyce, Canada • **1984** David Jensen and Bob Mason, United States • **1980** Steve Janaszak and Mark Wells, United States

---

Wells and Janaszak won gold medals in 1980, Ratushny won silver in 1992, Schreiber won silver in 1992 and 1994, and Butsayev won a gold medal in 1992.

Bobby Jay was an assistant coach with the 2014 U.S. women's team, which won a silver medal in Sochi.

CHAPTER 12

Boileau created great memories in Fort Wayne

Marc Boileau will always be remembered in Fort Wayne for winning, but in the NHL he's remembered for something else.

Though he played 54 games with the Detroit Red Wings in 1961-62, Boileau was known as a journeyman minor leaguer when he came to the Komets as a center from the Western Hockey League's Seattle Totems in 1970. He played two seasons, becoming the team's head coach early in the 1970-71 season and the Komets' last full-time player-coach. That squad finished 23-24-12 under Boileau, and the 1971-72 team finished 37-33-2.

In 1972-73, Boileau helped the Komets acquire players such as Brian Walker, Jimmy Pearson, Don Atchison, Bob Fitchner and Jeff Ablett from the Pittsburgh Penguins. The Komets were coasting along at 31-19-2 when they caught fire with 22 games left. They finished 17-4-1 over the last six weeks to win the South Division and the Huber Trophy as the International Hockey League's regular-season champions.

During the playoffs, the Komets beat Flint 4-1 in the first round as Fitchner challenged the Generals' bench in the first game. In the finals, they swept Port Huron 4-0, gaining revenge after getting knocked out of the playoffs by the Wings the year before.

This made Boileau one of the few people to win IHL championships as a player and coach; he also won a Turner Cup as a player with the Indianapolis Chiefs in 1958.

"It started with Marc," said Fitchner. "He did a lot of team building. He had built up respect. He was tough and demanding but also very fair. We just seemed to have a team where everybody got along. We did a lot of things together. We went bowling every Tuesday. All those things seem to build."

Boileau started the next season, 1973-74, behind the Komets' bench, but he was named coach of the National Hockey League's Penguins on Feb. 6, 1974. He coached the team until Jan. 17, 1976, when he was replaced by the man he had replaced, Ken Schinkel.

Among his highlights in Pittsburgh was his 66-61-24 record. The 1974-75 team set the franchise record for points in a season with 89, and that record stood until Mario Lemieux joined the club a decade later.

But the Penguins lost in the 1975 playoffs to the New York Islanders despite having a 3-0 lead in the series. It's one of the few times in professional sports history that a team has let its opponent rally from a 3-0 deficit to win a playoff series. Unfortunately for Boileau, that's what his NHL career became known for.

After he was fired midway through the 1975-76 season, Boileau became coach of the World Hockey Association's Quebec Nordiques. He led the Nordiques to the AVCO Cup, the WHA's version of the Stanley Cup.

"The NHL never took them seriously, and that cost the NHL a lot of money," Boileau said. "The WHA had to establish themselves right off the bat. The only thing feasible to look to the future was to get a few of the NHL established stars."

Marc Boileau celebrates the 1973 Turner Cup in Port Huron. *Courtesy of The News-Sentinel*

Boileau coached two years in Quebec, compiling a 74-61-5 record. After that, he coached the Flint Generals in the IHL and then coached in Holland and France. He retired to Montreal in 1995 and served as a goal judge at the Molson Centre.

He died Dec. 27, 2000, after suffering a massive heart attack while playing hockey with a group of kids on a lake in his hometown of Pointe Claire, Quebec.

CHAPTER 13

WHA challenged, shaped the NHL game

At one time, former Komets Bob Fitchner, Marc Boileau and John Ferguson were readjusting their careers after being NHL outlaws. The 1979-80 season was the first for former World Hockey Association teams Edmonton, Quebec, Winnipeg and Hartford to play in the NHL.

Fitchner, the captain of the Komets' 1973 Turner Cup championship team, was a forward with the Quebec Nordiques. Ferguson, the first Komets player to make it to the NHL, was the general manager of the WHA champion Winnipeg Jets. Boileau, coach of the Komets' 1973 Turner Cup team, was out of a job as coach of the Nordiques despite leading them to the WHA title two years earlier. He returned to the IHL to coach Flint.

Like the American Football League and American Basketball Association before it, the WHA started because some cities wanted NHL teams and could not get them. The NHL was a 16-team league in 1972-73, but the only Canadian cities included were Montreal, Toronto and Vancouver. Edmonton, Winnipeg and Quebec became the heart of the WHA.

"The NHL never took them seriously, and that cost the NHL a lot of money," said Boileau. "The WHA had to establish themselves right off the bat. The only thing feasible to look to the future was to get a few of the NHL established stars."

The WHA signed the Chicago Blackhawks' Bobby Hull to a 10-year, $1.75 million contract in the summer of 1972, which was considerably more than Chicago's offer of $100,000 for one season. In 1970, the average NHL salary was $22,000.

"Boom, all of a sudden the salaries started to go up," Boileau said.

The WHA also signed NHL stars such as Gordie Howe, Dave Keon and Gerry Cheevers. The money was too good to turn down.

"The league created a lot of excitement," said Fitchner, a high school social studies teacher in Carman, Manitoba. "It gave a lot of players that maybe didn't have the opportunity to play in the NHL more opportunities to play at the major league level."

Fitchner played seven years in the WHA with Edmonton, Indianapolis and Quebec as a checking forward, which meant he played against some great players.

"One of the biggest things for me was I had a chance to play against guys I never imagined I'd have the opportunity to play with," Fitchner said. "People like Howe, Hull, Keon. I never expected to be on the same ice surface with those individuals."

Fitchner still has a picture of himself working the puck behind the net with Howe in pursuit.

During the 1977 playoffs, Fitchner's line matched up against Winnipeg's superstar line of Hull, Ulf Nilsson and Anders Hedberg. The NHL's Toronto Maple Leafs had recruited Borje Salming from Sweden to play in 1973, but European players were rare and were never stars. To compete for talent, the WHA aggressively signed European players in the mid-1970s.

The WHA also started signing junior players and gave players such as Wayne Gretzky, Mark Messier and Mike Gartner their professional starts. Messier was the last active NHL player with WHA experience.

Bob Fitchner
Courtesy of The News-Sentinel

"People like that really made the league into a very, very quality league," said Ferguson. "It had a lot of good, young players. There was no question in my mind in the last year of the WHA, we won the AVCO Cup in Winnipeg, and we would have given the Montreal Canadiens a pretty good run."

Like Julius Erving in the ABA, Gretzky became a key to forcing the NHL to merge with the WHA.

"The man without a doubt had ice vision beyond anybody else," Ferguson said. "He was like a good pool shooter knowing where the next shot was going to be. He could see the ice, and he just made plays with the ability to stay out of trouble and make passes."

Among the other former Komets who played in the league are Paul Hoganson, Mike Boland, Bruce Boudreau, Jeff Carlson, Randy Legge, Bernie MacNeil, Dwayne Pentland, Duane Rupp and Paul Shmyr. Tom McVie also coached one year for Ferguson in Winnipeg and led the Jets to the 1978-79 AVCO Cup.

Komets who won WHA AVCO Cups

Marc Boileau
Quebec Nordiques coach, 1977

Bob Fitchner
Quebec Nordiques, 1977

John Ferguson
Winnipeg Jets general manager, 1979

Tom McVie
Winnipeg Jets coach, 1979

CHAPTER 14

White broke color barrier with Komets, pro hockey

As a kid growing up in Winnipeg, Alton White never experienced racism, though his was the only black family in the neighborhood. It was a cosmopolitan area full of immigrants.

"We read about it in the paper, but you'd say, 'Does that really happen?'" White said. "I always hung around with my buddies who were all white kids and never thought anything of it. I was always treated pretty well."

White came to Fort Wayne as a rookie in 1965 to play for the Komets. He was the first black player to play for the Komets, though there had been a couple in the International Hockey League before, including Ray Leacock with Cincinnati and Art Dorrington with Johnstown in the early 1950s.

But the Komets had never integrated before. General Manager Ken Ullyot recruited White and his buddy Ken Sutyla out of a New York Rangers prospect camp in St. Paul, Minn.

"I had to go out and look for a place to live, and that was the first time I ever ran into discrimination," White recalled. "Hank Kernohan was a real hockey fan and a good guy, and he took us under his wing and was showing us around. The first place he took us to, we really liked the apartment and were really eager, but the lady kind of backed around the corner so I couldn't hear, and she told them no, I couldn't live there because I was black.

Alton White
Courtesy of Fort Wayne Komets

"That just hurt."

It was a rude introduction to professional hockey, but White and Sutyla eventually found a house on South Anthony Boulevard between Pontiac Street and Creighton Avenue with goaltender Gerry Randall.

"There were some problems I found sometimes when people looked at him a bit funny, but he didn't understand it because it was his first time out of Canada," Sutyla said. "We just ignored it."

Besides finding housing, and despite some early homesickness, White also found a hockey home with the Komets, where he scored 17 goals and 42 points in 62 games. His teammates never thought anything about the color of his skin.

"It was not a big deal for us because we had all played with him in Canada," all-time Komets scoring leader Len Thornson said.

Eddie Long, who coached the team that season, described White as "a real gentleman, really a nice guy who was a hard worker. He didn't want anything he didn't earn."

It helped that Sutyla was also on the team, at least for the first half of the season. They teamed with Chick Balon on a forward line. After Sutyla left, White spent time on a line with Thornson and Colin Longmuir.

"It was really a great experience for me to see how everybody handled themselves," White said. "Lionel Repka took us under his wing and taught us all the time to help us get better. My

Fort Wayne teammates were wonderful, and I learned a lot from them about being a pro, and I grew up a little, too."

The funny thing? In 1971, the movie Brian's Song highlighted the fact that Gale Sayers and Brian Piccalo were supposedly among the first interracial roommates. But White and Sutyla, who had been friends since they were 14 or 15 in Winnipeg, had roomed together years earlier.

"We never thought anything of it," White said.

White stood up in Sutyla's wedding, and they are still good friends today.

"He was such a nice guy and got along with everybody," Sutyla said. "He was just a great athlete and a very likable guy."

After the 1965-66 season, the Komets lost White to Des Moines in the intra-league draft, but White's career was about to take off. He bounced to the Columbus Checkers for three seasons before signing with Providence from the American Hockey League.

That's when White got his big break as he was drafted in the first round by the new World Hockey Association's New York Raiders. On Oct. 12, 1972, White became the second black player to play in a major league game (after Willie O'Ree, who played two games with the Boston Bruins in 1957-58 and 43 with the Bruins in 1960-61).

After 13 games, White was traded to the Los Angeles Sharks, where he became the first black player to score 20 goals in a season and the first to score a hat trick, notching three goals in seven minutes against the Minnesota Fighting Saints on March 1, 1973. He finished with 21 goals and 42 points in 60 games.

The next season, he was troubled by a cut on his leg and was limited to eight goals and 21 points in 48 games. In the season that followed, he bounced between the North American Hockey League's Syracuse Blazers and the WHA's Michigan Stags/ Baltimore Blades.

And then White retired. He went home to Winnipeg and then moved to Vancouver where he joined his three brothers' construction business. He's still there today. He and Linda will celebrate their 50th wedding anniversary in 2019.

The only thing White didn't get to accomplish was playing in the NHL. While he played with Providence of the AHL, other players got called up, but he never did.

"When I was in Providence, we were affiliated with Oakland, and I'd have a pretty good training camp, but I always got sent down," White said. "I just never got the call. There were a lot of guys up there who I was a better hockey player than, but I never rocked the boat. I just played as well as I could."

Was it because of racism?

"I hate to say that, but..." he said.

At one time, White had a discussion with two well-respected and long-time hockey front-office officials who told him, "If we called you up and something happened, we'd feel real bad if we had to send you back down. Don't think we're not calling you up because of this or that."

That was the only discussion he ever had with an NHL front-office person.

"I'm not bitter," he said. "I met some great people, and hockey has benefited me big-time. When I quit hockey, I was pretty well-known around Vancouver, and when it came to business, it opened a lot of doors for me and for our company. My career started a lot of conversations."

Komets who played in the WHA

Les Binkley Ottawa, Toronto
Bill Blackwood Indianapolis
Bruce Boudreau Minnesota
Jim Boyd Phoenix, Calgary
Jeff Carlson Minnesota
Mike Federko Houston
Bob Fitchner Edmonton, Indianapolis, Quebec
Marty Gateman New England
Paul Hoganson Los Angeles, Michigan, Baltimore, Cincinnati, Indianapolis
Ron Hansis Houston
Mike Jakubo Los Angeles
Randy Legge Michigan, Baltimore, Winnipeg, Cleveland, San Diego
Ken Lockett San Diego
Al MacKenzie Chicago
Bernie MacNeil Los Angeles, Cincinnati
Dunc McCallum Houston, Chicago
Dave Morrow Indianapolis
Jim Park Indianapolis
Rusty Patenaude Edmonton, Indianapolis
Dwayne Pentland Houston
Lorne Rombough Chicago
Duane Rupp Vancouver, Calgary
Jim Shaw Toronto
Paul Shmyr Cleveland, San Diego, Edmonton
Garry Swain New England
Greg Tebbutt Birmingham
Carl Wetzel Minnesota
Alton White New York, Los Angeles, Michigan, Baltimore

CHAPTER 15

Irons helped change NHL in one appearance

On June 13, 1968, the Rangers traded Robbie Irons and Camille Henry to the expansion St. Louis Blues for Bill Plager, Don Caley and Wayne Rivers. Blues coach Scotty Bowman was building a goaltending tandem of future Hall of Famers Jacques Plante, 39, and Glenn Hall, 37.

"I met Scotty Bowman in downtown Toronto, and he told me he wanted to sign three young goaltenders to back up Glenn Hall and Jacques Plante," Irons said. "I was all for it. Scotty was always thinking outside the box. He knew he had two older guys and he needed to cut down on the travel time or it was going to wear them out."

Bowman signed Irons, Gary Edwards and Ted Oimet, sending two of them to play with the Blues' farm team in Kansas City while the other would serve as a practice goalie and back up either Plante or Hall during road games. If the Blues had a weekend road trip to Minnesota and Chicago, Plante or Hall would go straight to Chicago to wait for the team while Irons backed up the other in Minnesota. The season was split into thirds as the three goalies rotated, with Irons starting the first third in St. Louis.

Irons, 21, practiced every day and dressed with the Blues for more than 60 games over the next three seasons, wearing either No. 1 or No. 30 depending on whom he was backing up (taking the other goaltender's number).

"You just had to bide your time," Irons said.

His time came on Nov. 13, 1968, appropriately enough in a game at New York against the Rangers. The Blues and Plante had played the night before in Boston, so Hall was in net when the Rangers' Vic Hatfield ripped a long slap shot that dipped under Hall's arm and into the goal. Hall charged out to protest that Hatfield's stick had to be illegal, and he bumped into the referee to earn a game misconduct.

The referee skated to the St. Louis bench to tell Bowman to get his backup into the game. Bowman walked over to Irons and told him to take his time during the warm-up and then come back to the bench to see him. After a regular warm-up, which was permitted at the time, Irons came to the bench, and Bowman instructed him to go with the trainer into the locker room with a supposed leg injury.

"The trainer is messing around when Scotty comes in yelling at the referee, who says, 'C'mon, let's go. You gotta go,'" Irons said. "I don't really know what's going on other than I'm antsy and the building is jam-packed. So finally, out I come and the crowd is going crazy. They finally get me in the net, and we get started. I handled the puck a couple of times, and I think I might have made one save. Before I know it, three and a half minutes later, I look over and who's standing on the bench dressed but Jacques Plante, who had been sitting in the stands. Scotty calls me over, and in Jacques Plante goes. Then they give him a warm-up."

Bowman came down to the end of the bench and told Irons he did a good job. The Blues won 2-1, but the Rangers started a huge argument with the league office that led to a rule change. After that game, teams were limited to the two goaltenders listed on the lineup card.

"As a young kid, I didn't know how I would handle it, but when I went in, I was shaking in my boots, there's no doubt about it," Irons said. "The fooling around upset me from the standpoint of, 'C'mon, let's get going, I don't need this Mickey Mouse stuff. If I'm going to play, let's go. If I'm going to fall on my face, fine. Let's get this thing going.' Once I got in there and actually handled the puck, I started to relax and feel OK."

The next year, Irons played three exhibition games with St. Louis but never got into another NHL game. He holds a record with Christian Soucy and Sean Gauthier for least minutes played (three) in a career by an NHL goaltender.

He played 60 games over the next three seasons in Kansas City as Oimet and Edwards took their turns in St. Louis. Oimet played in one game with the Blues and Edwards in two during that time.

The only problem came during the third season when Bowman moved Irons back and forth to Kansas City several times, which was frustrating for all three goaltenders, who had no idea what Bowman was trying to do.

One day in 1970, Henry was coaching Kansas City and called Irons into the office to tell him there was going to be a major shakeup the next day, but that Bowman had told him Irons would be fine. So the next day, Irons was called to the phone to talk with Bowman who said, "Robbie, I'm sorry but I don't have

Robbie Irons

Courtesy of The News-Sentinel

a job for you. Get your expenses together and see me when you come back to St. Louis."

Upset, Irons flew to St. Louis with itemized expenses for $2,800. That enraged Bowman, who argued over every nickel. Irons eventually got his money. He never played in another NHL game, but the story doesn't end there.

After leaving Bowman in his St. Louis office in 1970, Irons came back to Fort Wayne, where Marc Boileau had just taken over as Komets coach and Jimmy Keough was in his second year manning the Fort Wayne nets. Irons was an immediate improvement, cutting a goal per game off the Komets' defensive average.

Near the end of Irons' career in 1980, he received a call one

September day from Komets General Manager Ken Ullyot to come to the office. Ullyot had taken a call from Blues General Manager Emile Francis who wanted to talk to Irons. Ironically, Francis had been the Rangers' general manager during the 1968 game and had led the New York protest to the league.

"It jumps in my head right away that they want me to go to training camp," Irons said. "He gets on the phone and says, 'We've got an oldtimers game in Chicago, and we need a goaltender. Glenn Hall is going to play for Chicago.' I said, 'Wow, you must have looked a long ways down the list,' and he said, 'Robbie, you're on the list and that's all that matters.'"

Irons agreed and drove to Chicago with a buddy the next day to play on Sunday before the Komets opened training camp on Monday. He walked into the dressing room and saw Bowman standing there along with some of his former teammates.

There was a full house because Bobby Hull was dressing in a Blackhawks uniform for the first time in 10 years. Bob Johnson played in goal for St. Louis during the game's first half, and Chicago was leading 2-0 when Irons went in. The Blackhawks had the extra attacker in the final seconds, but Irons made some big saves. He shut out Chicago the rest of the ways as the Blues ended up winning 3-2.

Irons has a picture of himself playing in the game wearing his Komets mask while Hull and the Blackhawks' Red Hay are battling in front of him with a St. Louis defenseman.

"So we win the game and I go into the dressing room, and Scotty greeted me and said, 'You're still playing? You still got a couple more years in you?' I said, 'Any time.'"

During the 1994 NHL lockout, Bowman, who was coaching the Detroit Red Wings at the time, showed up to watch a game in Fort Wayne at Memorial Coliseum. Irons was broadcasting with Bob Chase.

"I got off the radio and we talked a little bit," Irons said. "He says, 'There's never been a goaltender who knew what the hell he was talking about on radio. I'll have to listen on the way back home.'"

Same old Scotty.

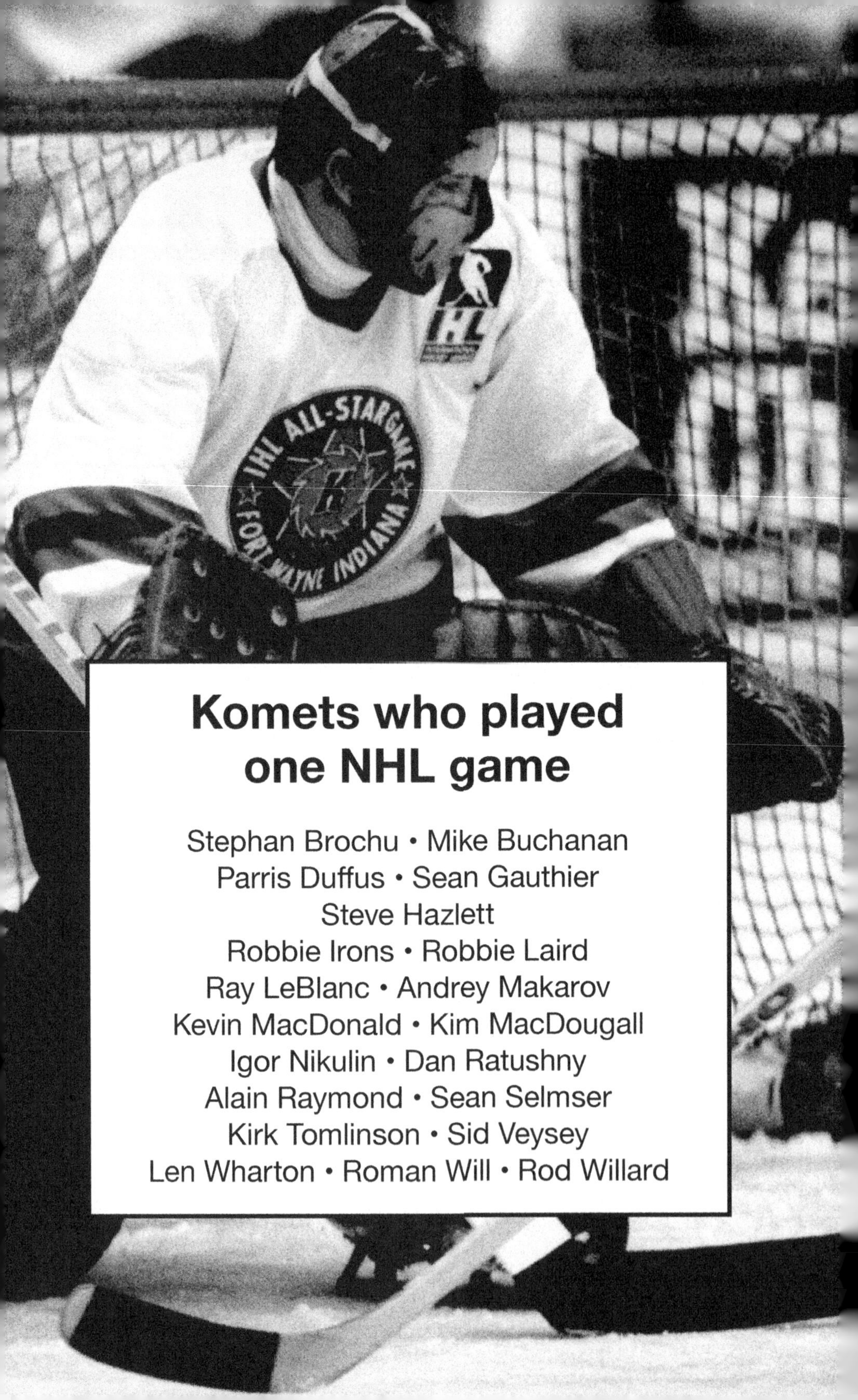

Komets who played one NHL game

Stephan Brochu • Mike Buchanan
Parris Duffus • Sean Gauthier
Steve Hazlett
Robbie Irons • Robbie Laird
Ray LeBlanc • Andrey Makarov
Kevin MacDonald • Kim MacDougall
Igor Nikulin • Dan Ratushny
Alain Raymond • Sean Selmser
Kirk Tomlinson • Sid Veysey
Len Wharton • Roman Will • Rod Willard

CHAPTER 16

Fort Wayne has become home for goalies

The Los Angeles Lakers are known for getting all-star centers in trades, the New York Yankees for developing classic outfielders and the Chicago Bears for drafting great linebackers.

During their 65-year history, the Fort Wayne Komets have been known for cultivating outstanding goaltenders.

Fort Wayne fans have watched 29 former Komets netminders advance to the National Hockey League, by far the most Fort Wayne players to make the NHL at any one position. That number is amazing considering the Komets didn't get their first netminders to the NHL until Les Binkley and Roy Edwards in 1967, the year the NHL expanded from six teams to 12. Over their last 20 years in the International Hockey League (which ended in 1999), the Komets had 22 of their former goalies play in the NHL.

That list does not include players such as Tim Cheveldae, Peter Ing, Bruce Racine, Rick St. Croix or Ron Loustel, who all played in Fort Wayne after playing in the NHL for the last time. Nor does it include Jim Shaw, Jim Park, Carl Wetzel or Dan LaPointe, who played in the World Hockey Association, or the great Chuck Adamson, a career minor leaguer who won two Turner Cups.

Such an extensive list is due in part to NHL expansion, which began in 1967. And it is helped by Komets equipment manager Joe Franke, who babies goaltenders with special treatment and attention, taking care of them as if they were his own children.

But there are other reasons, too.

"I think the first thing that impressed me when I came here was Memorial Coliseum," said Robbie Irons, who holds most Komets career records. "Coming to that building, the good-sized crowds gave you a lot of enthusiasm."

The lighting in the coliseum is good, and there are few odd bounces off the boards.

"I used to have a lot of goalies tell me they didn't like to play in Kalamazoo," former Komets player and coach Robbie Laird said. "The stands had those dark seats, and the boards were livelier."

Another factor in Fort Wayne's goalie success is that starting in the early 1970s, the Komets began a history of getting affiliations with National Hockey League clubs. NHL teams regularly signed more goaltenders than they could use, and the Komets benefited from players such as Pokey Reddick, Bob Essensa, Rick Tabaracci, Rick Knickle, Stephane Beauregard, Tom Draper, Peter Sidorkiewcz and later Kevin Weekes.

"The only thing I can say is that they matured here and they didn't give up," longtime Komets General Manager Ken Ullyot said. "A lot of them didn't see the value of the IHL when they were sent here, but (they) eventually saw the competition and the opportunity, and they realized it was a good opportunity. It's almost like they woke up when they got here. They knew they had to work their tail off to last in the IHL."

Peter Sidorkiewicz
Courtesy of The News-Sentinel

It helped that the Komets, under coaches such as Ron Ullyot, Al Sims, John Torchetti, Greg Puhalski and Laird, stressed strong defensive systems. It also helped that the Komets' history created a strong tradition, Irons said.

"If none of the goalies from Fort Wayne ever got to the NHL, that would fall on everybody," he said. "The history has followed right through, and every goalie comes here with the idea that Murray Bannerman and the rest of them made it to the NHL, so maybe they can."

Komets goaltenders who later played in the NHL

NHL games played through the start of the 2017-18 season

Goaltender	Games
Bob Essensa	446
Kevin Weekes	348
Murray Bannerman	289
Rick Tabaracci	287
Peter Sidorkiewicz	246
Roy Edwards	236
Alain Chevrier	234
Les Binkley	196
Pokey Reddick	132
Bob Janecyk	110
Stephane Beauregard	90
Tom Draper	53
Frederic Chabot	32
Darren Jensen	30
Mike O'Neill	21
Rick Knickle	14
Don Cutts	6
Darrell May	6
Steve Janaszak	3
Spencer Martin	3
Paul Hoganson	2
Dave Gagnon	2
Richard Shulmistra	2
Alain Raymond	1
Ray LeBlanc	1
Sean Gauthier	1
Robbie Irons	1

CHAPTER 17

Komets had fun with Stanley Cup

Maybe it's because the players have to sacrifice so much to earn it, or because it's the longest-lasting trophy in team sports, or maybe it's simply because it's one of the few trophies that players get to have their names engraved on, but the National Hockey League's Stanley Cup is the icon for all professional sports trophies.

There are 13 Komets who have gone on to win the cup, and all of them have fascinating stories to add to its lore.

Who was one of the first stars to immediately announce his retirement after winning the cup? Remember the end of the New York Islanders' and Edmonton Oilers' dynasties? Ever wonder what happened to the puck Brett Hull scored with in overtime of Game 6 in 1999? How about how the tradition started of players getting individual time with the cup?

Komets were involved in all of that.

John Ferguson, the first Komet to make it to the NHL, became one of the first and most likely the quickest player to hang up his skates after winning a Stanley Cup. Minutes after his 1971 Montreal Canadiens beat the Chicago Blackhawks in Game 7, Ferguson said he was quitting at age 32.

Ferguson leads the list of former Komets with five Stanley Cup titles, ahead of Gord Lane with four, and Shawn Chambers and Hector Marini with two.

"Nowadays you don't play for the team logo anymore, but you play for the dollar sign," Ferguson said in 2002. "Despite that, the cup still has great meaning. Most of the free agents now say they won't play with anyone unless they have a chance to win the Stanley Cup."

The NHL purchased the cup in 1893 for about $50 and started awarding it to its champion in 1927. More than 1,000 people have had their names inscribed on it. The cup is insured for $75,000 but has been estimated to be worth more than $3 million.

"I don't know exactly how heavy it is, but when I first lifted it, it's heavier than you ever imagined," Chambers said. "It takes you by surprise. You don't feel it right there when you are on the ice. You know it's a little heavy, but afterward you start to realize how heavy it is."

The celebration of a title starts as soon as the game ends. Chambers was on the ice for the end both times he won the cup, in 1995 with New Jersey and in 1999 with Dallas.

"The first time, the puck went behind the net and I was talking to (goaltender Martin) Brodeur," Chambers said. "Everybody was hugging him, and I saw the puck behind the net, so I grabbed it."

That was good preparation for the 1999 title. Seconds after Hull scored his controversial overtime goal to beat Buffalo, Chambers grabbed the puck in the corner and shoved it down his pants. One of the most famous pucks in hockey history is on top of Chambers' television set in northern Minnesota.

"We are in the midst of building a new house," Chambers said in 2002. "Once I get in there I'll figure out what I want to do with (the two pucks). Those are about the only souvenirs I have."

Chambers also had the task of taking the cup home to Detroit after the Devils had beaten the Red Wings in the Stanley Cup Finals.

"The only people in Detroit rooting for me were from my family, and not even all of them," he said. "My uncles are huge die-hard Red Wings fans. It was fun."

Marini also had fun with the cup. He was part of the New York Islanders' four Stanley Cup teams in 1981 and 1982.

"Sometimes I think I'm still celebrating," he said.

Marini did not play in either final game, though he scored nine points in nine games to help the Islanders get to the finals in 1981. He was filling in for Duane Sutter who returned to the lineup after recovering from an injury.

"The great thing that I can remember is that Jimmy Devellano – the guy who scouted me and believed in me when no one else did – and I took the cup on a cruise around Manhattan," Marini said. "We managed to take the cup, and no one noticed. It was just the two of us with the cup sitting between us for a couple of hours. We had dinner and drinks and then took it back."

Marini gave his first Stanley Cup ring to his father and kept the second, though he rarely wears it. Lane, Marini's former teammate, was part of all four championship New York teams.

"The biggest thing I remember was not so much the satisfaction of winning it, but the satisfaction that it was over," Lane said. "It was such a grueling thing."

The Islanders' run ended in 1984 when the Edmonton Oilers started their streak of five cups in seven years. When their reign ended in 1990, Pokey Reddick was the backup goaltender. He is the only Komet to win both the Stanley Cup and Turner Cup.

"You can't even describe it, you just have to go through it," Reddick said. "It's almost as if by trying to describe it you are cheating yourself. It's almost like having your first kid. It's awesome."

During his day with the cup, he took pictures of 3-year-old son Bryce sitting in it. Then Reddick sat down to read all the names and think about all the history associated with them.

One of those names was Ferguson, who said that during his career, the players were not allowed to take the cup for a day. The Montreal players were able to see it at a windup party at city hall, and that was it. The next day, the players spent the afternoon at coach Toe Blake's tavern.

The post-game parties are now a tradition. In 1991, while working for Pittsburgh's Muskegon farm team, current Komets equipment manager Joe Franke was helping the Penguins during the playoffs. As the Penguins celebrated winning their first title in Minnesota, Franke was on the ice helping to pick up equipment, part of which belonged to Randy Gilhen and Grant Jennings.

Paul Coffey and Joe Franke

Courtesy of Pittsburgh Penguins

"At the end of the whole thing, we got to hold the cup and get our picture taken with it," Franke said. "When it came off the airplane, I don't know how we made it through the airport. It was like a gauntlet. They had to have crowd control all the way to Mario's (Lemieux) house."

Gilhen was finishing his last shift of the game when the final horn went off. Because Pittsburgh beat Minnesota 8-0, the end was somewhat anticlimactic. He knew just what to do when Jimmy Paek passed him the cup.

"I wanted to take it over to the guys who hadn't played," Gilhen said. "They were just standing there on the ice, but they had played a big part in that team, too."

That group included Jennings, who also won the cup again with the Penguins a year later. That is when the cup sank to the bottom of Lemieux's pool.

A year after that, Franke was helping the Komets put the International Hockey League's Turner Cup back together after it was run over by a forklift when a player dropped it.

Former Komets coach John Torchetti said his favorite memory from the 2010 celebration was watching his mother get her picture taken with the trophy and his father getting doused with champagne.

"What I've been working for my whole life was that cup," Torchetti said. "Everything that I worked so hard for was all worth it times 50 when I got to kiss it."

Los Angeles Kings scout Rob Laird shared the cup with Fort Wayne as a crowd of about 2,000 fans showed up to have their picture taken with the trophy. Laird and his wife Madeleine were expecting around 300.

"I love the fact that Fort Wayne has shown their passion for hockey with this turnout," Laird said.

Eventually, the parties end and the cup goes back to the Hockey Hall of Fame in Toronto with the names of 24 to 26 new players engraved on it.

"I still have the tapes of the finals, and I often have some of my buddies over to watch them," Lane said. "Even my daughters, who never saw me play, will sit and watch them. I find myself getting as involved in them now as I did 20-some years ago. It's just a lot of fun to sit there and watch and feel it all over again."

Gilhen got to feel that again a few years ago when he and a friend toured the Hall of Fame in Toronto and looked at the cup.

"It's one of those trophies that every player who has won it feels like they own a part of it," Gilhen said. "You remember all those little memories that go on. It's a pretty special feeling."

Komets who have won the Stanley Cup

John Ferguson Montreal Canadiens
1965, 1966, 1968, 1969, 1971

Shawn Chambers New Jersey Devils, 1995, Dallas Stars, 1999

Joe Franke Pittsburgh Penguins trainer, 1991

Pokey Reddick Edmonton Oilers, 1990

Gord Lane New York Islanders
1980, 1981, 1982, 1983

Hector Marini New York Islanders, 1981, 1982

Randy Gilhen Pittsburgh Penguins, 1991

Grant Jennings Pittsburgh Penguins, 1991, 1992

Andre Roy Tampa Bay Lightning, 2004

John Torchetti Chicago Blackhawks assistant coach, 2010

Clint Reif Chicago Blackhawks equipment manager, 2010

Bob Essensa Boston Bruins goalie coach, 2011

Rob Laird Los Angeles Kings senior pro scout, 2012, 2014

CHAPTER 18

Marini moved on to new career after losing his eye

When he heard about the Montreal Canadiens' Trent McCleary getting hit by a slap shot in late January 2000, Hector Marini left his job as a corrections officer at the Toronto West Detention Center to rush home and watch the TV replay. McCleary, a 27-year-old center, was hit in the throat while diving to block a slap shot in a game against the Philadelphia Flyers.

"I was looking at it, and he gets back up, but when he threw his gloves away and didn't care where they landed, I knew it was serious," Marini said. "I really felt for him."

Because of a fractured larynx, McCleary could not breathe and required an emergency tracheotomy. The injury ended his career.

Marini can understand because he went through something similar. On Dec. 5, 1985, while playing for the Komets, Marini was trying to gain position in front of the Indianapolis Checkers' net on a power play when teammate Doug Rigler tried a slap shot from near the blue line. The puck hit Marini's left eye, and he crumpled to the Market Square Arena ice.

"The way I was bent over, the puck just hit me flush," Marini said. "I knew when it hit me that this was serious stuff. This was like someone raised the bar on pain."

The first person to reach Marini was current Komets hockey

trainer Joe Franke, who at the time was working for the Checkers.

"You could hear it," Franke said. "We took him off the ice and into our dressing room, and they held up play for a long time.'"

Hector Marini
Courtesy of New York Islanders

Unlike every player today, Marini was not wearing a protective visor, because as he said, "You never wore visors because it was a macho thing. You just didn't do it."

Doctors said his retina was detached, and four days later, they had to remove the eye. Marini's hockey career, which included two Stanley Cup championships with the New York Islanders, was finished at age 28 after only seven games with the Komets.

The New Jersey Devils, whose contract he was under at the time, offered Marini a scouting job, but he wanted out of hockey. He went to school for one year at Keane College in New Jersey and then studied international traffic and customs for three years at Seneca College in Toronto.

He had majored in international traffic and customs, but after he graduated in 1990, the job offers weren't great. Marini was spending time with former teammate Jim Park, and Park's sister, a corrections officer, persuaded Marini to fill out an application.

Today, Marini and his wife, Nancy, have been married for 30 years and live in Mississauga, Ontario. They have a son, Ryan, and a daughter, Alexandra. Marini even resumed playing after a while, wearing a full mask as he played with the corrections facility's team in a no-contact league.

"Here I am, 43 years old, trying to keep up with 21-year-olds," he said in 2000. "I have lots of fun."

Marini says he can talk and even express some morbid humor about what happened to him.

"You could say I kept my eye on the puck," he said, breaking into laughter. "I can laugh about it now, but when it happened, it took awhile. There were a lot of days where I was crying, but you have to move on. Everything worked out OK."

CHAPTER 19

Torchetti was always driven to make NHL

Whenever John Torchetti moved up a level in his minor league hockey coaching career, his father would visit from Boston. Once.

"The next time he comes to see me will be when I'm in the NHL," Torchetti said while coaching the Fort Wayne Komets in 1997-98.

It took him a few years, but eventually Torchetti made it, and his father came to visit. Once.

In 2010, Torchetti's parents made an exception to the rule for another visit, celebrating with the Stanley Cup in Philadelphia. Torchetti, then the associate coach of the Chicago Blackhawks, said he was so excited he couldn't remember who handed him the cup, but his favorite moments were watching his mother get her picture taken with the trophy and his father getting doused with champagne.

"You know my story and my life," Torchetti said. "What I've been working for my whole life was that cup. Everything that I worked so hard for was all worth it times 50 when I got to kiss it."

Everything in Torchetti's coaching life has been a challenge.

After retiring as a player in 1992, Torchetti started his coaching career as an intern with Greensboro of the Atlantic Coast Hockey League. The job paid nothing, so he bought a cab and drove 22 miles every day to Winston-Salem to scan for customers because, he said, "It was the only job I could find that would work around my coaching hours."

John Torchetti
Courtesy of Minnesota Wild

"One day, I'd leave after the morning skate and work until about 5 p.m., and hustle back to the rink by 5:20 p.m. Then after the game, I'd drive back at about 11:15 p.m. and work until 3 or 4 in the morning. I stayed out until I made X number of dollars each night. I always thought that if I wanted to be a coach, this was a test I had to pass."

It was a tough job. Torchetti developed a reputation as a driver who would go anywhere in the city to find customers, even into the projects or places where other drivers would not. There were often arguments and fights taking place in his back seat. One time a customer pulled a knife on him.

"That's a mark in my life where you played eight years pro and now you're driving a cab," Torchetti said. "I just look at it as you do what you have to to get by."

One time, Torchetti was driving with two men in the back seat when one fired a shot through the window at a man walking down the street. Torchetti, who carried a 9mm gun while he drove, pulled the cab over, ordered the men out, and then called the police as the men fled. Luckily, the shot missed.

"I had to pull the gun out sometimes," he said. "Some guys

thought they were going to be difficult customers, and I just told them I was a guy trying to do a job and make a living. There were a couple of times when people tried to rob me. There were some rough times, but I wanted to be a coach, and this is what I had to do."

Torchetti drove a cab for three years until he left Greensboro in 1994 to become the head coach of the Central Hockey League's San Antonio Iguanas at midseason. Then-Iguanas coach Bill Goldsworthy had just been diagnosed with AIDS.

Torchetti came to the Komets during the 1996-97 season as Dave Farrish's replacement. The Komets struggled through their worst season ever, but the next season, they rallied with a 37-point improvement to win a division title, and Torchetti was named the International Hockey League's Coach of the Year.

Since leaving the Komets after that season, Torchetti has bounced around the world of hockey. He has served as head coach with Florida, Los Angeles and Minnesota, and has worked as an assistant with Tampa Bay, Florida, Chicago and now Detroit. He also has coached four years in the American Hockey League and one year with CSKA Moscow, formerly the world-renowned Red Army Team.

"It was a chance to coach the most historic franchise and winning organization in Russia and possibly all of hockey, and also the opportunity to be a non-Russian coaching the Red Army Team," Torchetti said. "I always liked challenges in coaching."

Those challenges and those experiences, including driving the cab, became part of who he is.

"I've seen it all," he said. "Players have to pay a price to get to the NHL, and I had to pay a price. It makes me work harder every day. It also helped me to work on my people skills. I got to meet all kinds of people in all kinds of situations."

Recalling those days also helps Torchetti survive now when his teams struggle. A losing streak? That's nothing after having someone pull a knife or a gun on you.

"Driving a cab makes me appreciate coaching, and I want to do this the rest of my life," he said.

Komets currently working in the NHL (2017)

John Anderson Minnesota, assistant coach

Andy Bezeau Montreal, scout

Bruce Boudreau Minnesota, head coach

Dave Cameron Calgary, assistant coach

Frederic Chabot Minnesota, goaltending development coach

Craig Channell Minnesota, scout

Bob Essensa Boston, goaltending coach

Dirk Graham San Jose, scout

Dennis Holland Dallas, scout

Dusty Imoo Los Angeles, goaltender development

Bob Janecyk Ottawa, scout

Paul Jerrard Calgary, assistant coach

Rob Laird Los Angeles, senior pro scout

Bob Mason Minnesota, goaltending coach

Tom McVie Boston, scout

Claude Noel New Jersey, scout

Todd Reirden Washington, associate coach

Rick St. Croix Winnipeg, goaltending coach

John Torchetti Detroit, assistant coach

Scott White Dallas, assistant general manager

CHAPTER 20

McCauley left Komets to become NHL's top referee

Wes McCauley
Courtesy of Associated Press

After working his way up through the ECHL and the Colonial Hockey League, defenseman Wes McCauley thought his career was taking off when he joined the 1995-96 Fort Wayne Komets. It just took a different path.

After playing infrequently and getting sent down to the Colonial Hockey League a few times, McCauley wasn't too surprised when Komets coach Dave Farrish asked to talk to talk with him after only eight games in Fort Wayne. McCauley had scored just one goal as a Komet.

"I had played that weekend, and everything seemed to be going in the right direction, but after practice there was a message on my machine to come see him in his office," McCauley said. "I go over and we kind of chit chat about this and that, and we were talking about where I stand, and he said, 'There's a lot of scouts in the crowd, and your name got brought up.'"

That's intriguing, McCauley said.

"We were thinking with the NHL going to a two-referee system and your bloodlines," Farrish said, "and we think that you would make a great referee."

That's somewhat funny given that McCauley is now one of the NHL's best referees. He has worked the 2013-17 Stanley Cup Finals and the 2016 World Cup. There are probably Olympics and NHL All-Star Games in his future. During the biggest games, the NHL wants McCauley blowing the whistle.

He comes by it naturally because wearing stripes is skin-deep in McCauley's family. His father, John, who died at age 44 in 1989, was a referee and the NHL's director of officiating for 10 years; his uncle, Ron Finn, was an NHL referee until 2000; and his cousin, Sean Finn, was a linesman in the American Hockey League, the International Hockey League and the ECHL.

"His uncanny 'feel' for the game (almost a lost art) allowed for the expected playoff intensity to flourish in each game he called," former NHL referee Kerry Fraser wrote of McCauley on TSN.ca. "Most importantly, McCauley demonstrated the courage and good judgment to make the tough call at any point in the game regardless of the score or time. He did not put his whistle away!"

Everyone expected Wes McCauley to become an official, but that wasn't his first goal. He wanted to be a player, was a captain at Michigan State and then became a Detroit Red Wings eighth-round draft pick in 1990. After leaving the Komets and completing the season with Muskegon in the Colonial Hockey League, McCauley played for one year in Italy, but that only delayed the inevitable.

He kept running into veteran supervisors who knew his dad or his uncle and knew him from his younger days. They always talked about the need for more former players to pick up a whistle.

"Maybe it kind of came along at the right time," McCauley said.

That started his climb through the minors as a linesman and then a referee. Learning from veterans along the way, McCauley called ECHL, IHL and AHL finals games before jumping to the NHL in 2003. He became a full-time NHL referee in 2005.

His playing experience helped; he knew some of the players because he had competed against them either in college or the minors. He wasn't a total unknown, he knew how to communicate with players and coaches, and he had that feel for the game.

"The one thing I know is they all want to win," McCauley said. "They are competitive and the official is the guy whose job is to keep it fair and safe, and they look at us as keeping them from winning or losing. I also have a little empathy for the guys who are holding their sticks a little too tight. I get it."

He's also very good at leaving what happens on the ice inside the glass. There's always the next game to move on to. There are 33 referees and 33 linesmen in the NHL, and they work 73 games every season, always pushing themselves to compete so they can earn playoff berths as well and maybe earn a spot in the next round. Their job is to serve the game, but they also want to represent the group in the Stanley Cup Finals.

"If there's a Game 7, you want to be one of the four men stepping on the ice to do that game," McCauley said. "That would be the ultimate."

McCauley has called the games for 16 seasons so far, easily surpassing his father's mark of 442 games. He's currently over 800 games.

"I pinch myself that I still get to skate around," McCauley said. "Every year there's a new generation of kids coming in, and it's amazing ... how good the game is because they are getting better and better every year. It's neat because I'm a pretty lucky guy. I do my best to try and stay out of the highlights."

And it's all because of Dave Farrish and Fort Wayne. Until 2017, Farrish was an assistant coach with Colorado, and occasionally he'd yell at McCauley from the Avalanche bench to dispute a call.

"It's your fault!" McCauley yells back. "We always end up chuckling about it."

CHAPTER 21

Boudreau, Anderson predicted NHL partnership

The first time Bruce Boudreau met him, John Anderson was a 16-year-old red-haired right winger who had just been called up by the Ontario Hockey League's Toronto Marlboros. After watching Boudreau score 87 points with the Marlies the season before from the stands, Anderson thought the center was a superstar and knew to that in order to have a chance to score, he needed to play on the 18-year-old's line.

"I was lucky enough to assist on his first goal when he got up there," Boudreau said. "Then I assisted on his first NHL goal when he came up."

Except there's another story about that first NHL goal.

"It was against Minnesota, and Trevor Johansen scored his first goal, but Bruce got a hat trick that game and we won 6-3," Anderson recalls. "The funny thing was Gabby (Boudreau) didn't even get the first star (designation). He was so ticked off about it, and 40 years later, he's still ticked off. I'm like, 'Oh, my God, get over it!'"

A couple of years later while playing for the Toronto Maple Leafs, Boudreau and Anderson broke out on a 2-on-1 against the Boston Bruins. Knowing how good Boudreau was around the net, Anderson tried to set him up.

"It was kind of in his skates a little bit, and he couldn't handle it and shot it wide," Anderson said. "So we go back to the bench, and he looks at me and says, 'Thanks, you just got me sent down!' Sure enough, the next day he gets sent down.

"Honest to God, the paper had a picture of it, and he has that picture downstairs in his bar. Let it go, man! He tells this story to everybody, and he brings them down and shows them the picture, and then they kind of get where we're at."

Where they are at is behind the bench of the NHL's Minnesota Wild. In his third NHL coaching stint, Boudreau finished his first season as Minnesota's boss in 2016-17, and Anderson is his top assistant. For years as players they talked about playing together again at the end of their careers, which is why they came to Fort Wayne in 1990, and that entire season they talked about how someday they'd coach together in the NHL. Even when Boudreau was already an NHL coach in Washington and Anderson was leading the Atlanta Thrashers for two seasons, they never gave up on the dream. Though he had won four championships with the AHL's Chicago Wolves, Anderson resigned last summer as soon as Boudreau was named coach in Minnesota.

"It just took 27 years, can you imagine?" Anderson said. "He didn't have to convince me, all he had to do was ask me. The beautiful thing about Bruce is he doesn't change. He is who he is. He's as honest as the day is long, and he's very accountable. One thing about coaching in the AHL, no matter how well you do, you'll never get a Stanley Cup ring."

So last year became a Minnesota rebirth season and one for Anderson and Boudreau to be coaching in the same place.

Bruce Boudreau and John Anderson
Courtesy of Minnesota Wild

"We talked about this a lot when we lived together that year in Fort Wayne," Boudreau said.

The 1990-91 team was known as the Vagabond Komets, a group of players that other teams had given up on who considered themselves the "Dirty Dozen" of hockey. A remarkable season advanced the team to the Turner Cup Finals and revitalized hockey in Fort Wayne. Before Anderson (then 34) got hurt in February, Boudreau (then 36), Anderson and linemate Lonnie Loach were the International Hockey League's leading scorers, called "The Century Club" because of their combined age and because it looked like they'd all score 100 points. Both Anderson and Boudreau still call that season one of the best years of their lives.

"It was one of the closest teams I ever played on," Anderson said. "I was pissed off about hockey and wanted to retire. I just felt that hockey had done me wrong and I could still play in the NHL. I was so angry that I didn't want to play anymore. Then Gabby called me and said, 'Why don't you come to Fort Wayne?' and I'm like, 'Where in the world is Fort Wayne?' The only reason I went there was to play with him, and it was an awesome, awesome experience. I'm so glad I did it, because it made me feel good about myself and the game."

Anderson left after that season, but Boudreau remained for one more before retiring to start his coaching career in Muskegon. He came back to coach the Komets to the Turner Cup Finals in 1994, and Anderson started his coaching career two years later in Winston-Salem and then Quad City.

"We were friendly adversaries," Boudreau said. "Every time I played him, I wanted to beat him worse than I wanted to beat anybody. I remember one game we won in overtime after scoring a couple of goals late to tie it up. The refereeing was bad, and I heard John going over to the ref after the game to start yelling at him, and I'm like skipping off the ice as fast as I could and laughing my butt off."

Even off the ice, they've always been close. Anderson is godfather to Boudreau's son, introduced Boudreau to his first wife and then was co-best man (with former Komet Stu Burnie) at his second wedding. It's kind of appropriate because they often argue like an old married couple, knowing just where to poke because they were either there for or know all the stories about one another.

When Boudreau wanted an assistant coach to run the Wild's power play and also have his back, he knew Anderson would be perfect. They are self-described hockey nerds who can talk about the game all the time.

John Anderson and Bruce Boudreau
Courtesy of Fort Wayne Komets

"It's funny that I'm in my 60s and John is in his late-50s when we finally get the chance to work together again," Boudreau said. "We hung on long enough to see it happen."

Now the duo can get after each other in person, and the rest of the coaching staff thinks they are nuts but love laughing along. Anderson says he's the lucky guy to be part of a staff that includes Scott Stevens, Darby Hendrickson and Bob Mason.

"They think we're crazy, and we think we're normal," Anderson said. "When we're together, I give it to him and he gives it to me, and we laugh all the time. We both know that our heart is in the right place because we both want to win. I have his back 100 percent."

And now there are more stories to create.

"My son who visited recently brought me this nice off-the-bone ham," Anderson said. "We have this special bread that is made in the rink here, so I went and grabbed four slices so I can have it with this ham. You know what he did? He hid my bread on me, like we're 17 years old or something! 'You stole my bread!' And he started laughing. But this is how well I know him – the first place I look I found it. It never stops."

Yes, being together again has made both men feel just like teenagers, and they are once again setting each other up – this time off the ice.

"It's just been a pleasure so far," Boudreau said. "He loves the game as much as I do, and it would be a great finishing story if we could win something together."

Komets who became NHL head coaches

Dave Allison Ottawa, 1995-96

John Anderson Atlanta, 2008-09 thru 2009-10

Marc Boileau Pittsburgh, 1973-74 thru 1975-76

Bruce Boudreau Washington, Anaheim, Minnesota, 2007-08 thru current

Dave Cameron Ottawa, 2014-15 thru 2015-16

Fred Creighton Atlanta, Boston, 1974-75 thru 1979-80

John Ferguson New York Rangers, Winnipeg, 1975-76 thru 1976-77, 1985-86

Gerard Gallant Columbus, Florida, Las Vegas, 2003-04 thru 2006-07, 2014-15 thru current

Dirk Graham Chicago, 1998-99

Tom McVie Washington, Winnipeg, New Jersey, 1974-75 thru 1991-92

Claude Noel Columbus, Winnipeg, 2009-10 thru 2013-14

Al Sims San Jose, 1996-97

John Torchetti Florida, Los Angeles, Minnesota, 2003-04 thru 2015-16

Komets who became WHA head coaches

Marc Boileau Quebec, 1976-77 thru 1977-78

Tom McVie Winnipeg, 1978-79

CHAPTER 22

"Anderson Game" still a Fort Wayne marvel

Other players have scored more goals or more points or put forth amazing efforts in key playoff moments, but none had the flair or the lasting legacy of John Anderson's effort on May 17, 1991. Say the "Anderson Game," and every Komets fan knows what it signifies.

Following a 5-4 overtime loss two nights earlier, the Komets trailed the Peoria Rivermen 3-0 in the International Hockey League's Turner Cup Finals heading to Memorial Coliseum for Game 4. After upsetting defending champion Indianapolis and division winner Kalamazoo in the first two rounds, this was to be the end of the Komets' rebirth season. The Rivermen were the best-ever minor league hockey team, and the Komets were beat up and out of bodies. There were 8,025 fans who showed up to say goodbye.

Then Anderson came out for warm-ups without his helmet, and the crowd started buzzing.

With 73 points, the 34-year-old right wing had been the IHL's leading scorer through the first 51 games, but a deep thigh bruise on his right leg suffered on Jan. 26 caused calcium deposits to form on top of the bone. X-rays later showed the buildup to be six inches long and about an inch thick, causing the muscle to snag on it.

"The first day after the hit, my leg swelled up so much I couldn't put my jeans on," Anderson said.

The 12-year NHL veteran managed to play occasionally in 12 more regular-season games, scoring eight goals mostly on spot power-play duty. Anderson continually iced the leg between periods, but finally it gave out completely and he had to sit out the playoffs.

Somehow the Komets kept surviving, surprising everyone, but even they knew Peoria was the better team by then. They needed something to give them hope.

"During those playoffs, in that final series, he could barely walk to the rink," said former NHL teammate and future NHL coach Bruce Boudreau, who was the Komets' second-leading scorer that season. "After we lost Game 3, I remember the morning skate, and John was flying. We couldn't believe that all of a sudden he felt so good. It was like a miracle."

Anderson walked into coach Al Sims' office and did some one-arm pushups to prove he was ready to play.

"I said, 'You think about it this afternoon, and I'll come ready to play,'" Anderson said.

Sims didn't make the final decision until 10 minutes before warm-ups.

Suddenly, the Komets were all excited about the game, particularly Anderson, who decided he wasn't going to wear his helmet. Because he had signed a professional contract before June 1, 1979, Anderson was not required to wear one.

"I was just trying to think of something to do to get the team

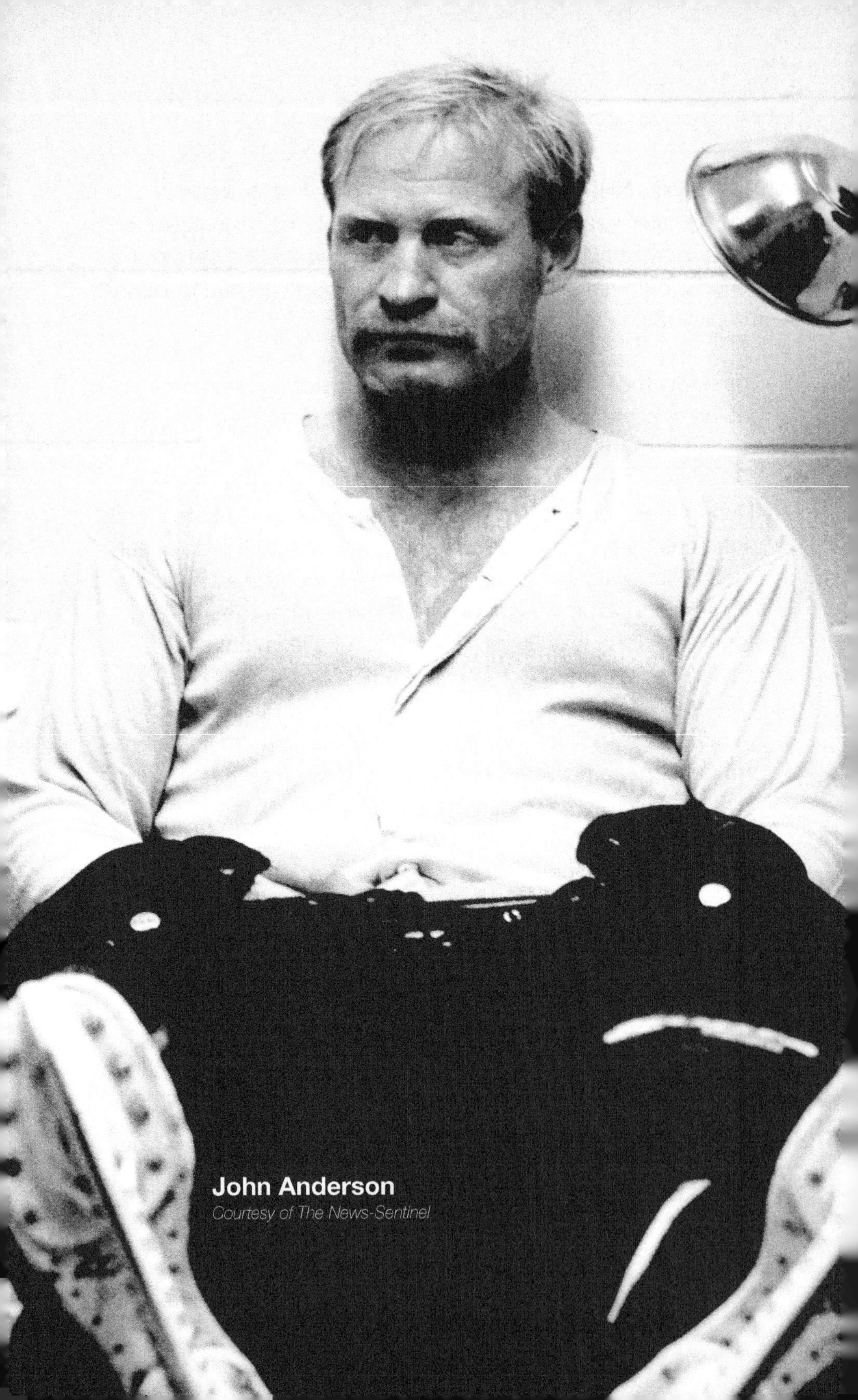

John Anderson
Courtesy of The News-Sentinel

sparked," Anderson said. "We were losing miserably, and Peoria was really good, so I wanted to do something different to take their mindset off being down 3-0."

Boudreau was so upset about Anderson not wearing a helmet, he called Anderson 's wife Karen in Hartford, Conn., from the training room.

"I was determined that if he was going to play, he was going to wear his helmet," Boudreau said. "It ended up nothing worked because he's a stubborn old goat."

Komets General Manager David Franke made Anderson sign a piece of paper as a waiver before taking the ice. No one in the building could believe what they were seeing, and then things just kept getting more incredible.

Anderson's first goal beat Peoria goalie Pat Jablonski and the clock, lighting the lamp at 19:59 of the first period to give the Komets a 2-1 lead and a huge lift. His second tally shocked everyone, particularly Jablonski, as Anderson rifled in a slap shot from 25 feet. The third came off a rebound, scooped over Jablonski when his defensemen failed to clear the puck.

Anderson showed flashes of everything – touch, hitting, slap shot and even speed – before taking a seat on the training room table for the third period. The score was 4-1 in the Komets' favor, and Anderson had earned a period of rest.

"My legs were like rubber out there," he said. "The first couple of shifts, my legs were shaking because I hadn't even been able to practice. After the two periods, I didn't have any legs left or anything."

Still, Anderson stayed in full uniform with his skates still laced up as he sat on the training table in case the Komets needed him again. They didn't, winning 5-2.

"That was probably the gutsiest performance by a Komet in many, many seasons," Franke said 20 years later. "We've had some guys play hurt since then, but before that morning, John Anderson could barely walk. The fact that he played so well is just amazing."

The performance was so remarkable, it was almost mystifying, as if no one could trust what they were seeing.

"I think the perseverance he showed that night with his leg and going helmet-less is just the stuff of Komets legend," Sims said. "You can just imagine the pain he was in and the lack of mobility with his leg. It was just an incredible thing."

Dave Eminian of the Peoria Journal-Star called Anderson the "thousand-year-old man" after the performance, but it gave the Komets new life. Anderson knew the leg wouldn't allow him to play again, but during the card game on the bus ride back to Peoria for Game 5, Boudreau said it was his turn to come up big. He did, scoring a hat trick to give the Komets a 4-3 win.

The Komets were sky-high coming into Game 6, but their sticks couldn't match their legs in a 3-1 loss with the game-winning goal going in off the leg of a Peoria forward.

Though his leg didn't fully recover until a month into the next season when he was playing with New Haven of the American Hockey League, Anderson played three more years before starting his coaching career, which led him back to the NHL with Atlanta. Now he's Boudreau's top assistant with the Minnesota Wild. He still hears from Komets fans occasionally about that miraculous night.

"It happened a couple of years ago in Atlanta," he said. "Somebody came up to me and said, 'I'm from Fort Wayne, and I remember that game.' I was kind of shocked."

Now he knows how everyone else felt that night.

The best of the 1-year-only Komets

Forwards

Name	Season
Luciano Acquino	2007-08
John Anderson	1990-91
Jim Baird	1960-61
Dan Bonar	1977-78
Mike Cazzola	2016-17
John Ferguson	1959-60
Randy Gilhen	1985-86
Bill Orban	1964-65
Dave Ross	1979-80
J.C. Ruid	2006-07
Rob Tudor	1976-77
Sid Veysey	1975-76

Defense

Name	Season
Chris Armstrong	1997-98
Mario Larocque	2006-07
Randy Legge	1966-67
Jim Leavens	1984-85
Al Sims	1988-89
Greg Tebbutt	1981-82

Goaltenders

Name	Season
Tim Haun	2009-10
Tom Lawson	2002-03

CHAPTER 23

Sims made it to NHL as player and coach

Al Sims

Courtesy of The News-Sentinel

As a rookie defenseman with the Boston Bruins in 1973, Al Sims already had a tough task in trying to make a team full of two-time Stanley Cup champions. And then he found out he was going to be partnered with all-time great Bobby Orr.

"When we started scrimmaging in training camp, I was with him, and the first time he had the puck, he circled around the net three times and nobody could catch him," Sims said. "I was just standing there on the other side of the ice watching him, like I'm watching him on TV or something, just in awe of him.

"Then he just fired a pass over to me, just shocked me and knocked the stick out of my hands. I think Phil Esposito got the puck and went in and scored, so of course I feel like an idiot coming back to the bench.

"Bobby just smacked me on the butt and said, 'Hey, you are a good enough player to be here. That's why you are here. Smarten up! Let's go!' I said, 'Yes, sir, Mr. Orr, no problem.' It's a pretty funny way to introduce yourself to Bobby Orr, screwing up like that."

Because Sims settled down and played well enough in training camp, veteran Don Awrey was traded to St. Louis to create a spot in the lineup. While Orr scored 32 goals and 122 points, Sims finished with three goals and 12 points as the Bruins were defeated in the Stanley Cup Finals by Philadelphia in six games.

The next season, 1974-75, Orr was even better with 46 goals and 135 points, while Sims had four goals and 12 points.

"He had had six operations on his knee by then, and he only lasted a couple of years after that," Sims said. "He was basically on one leg when I played with him, and he was still better than everybody else."

Orr played 10 games in 1975-76 before being traded to Chicago, but his career was essentially over while Sims' was just getting started. Sims played six seasons with the Bruins before going to Hartford for two seasons and then Los Angeles for nine games over two seasons. He finished with 476 games, 49 goals, 165 points and 40 playoff games. He was steady and dependable.

Extending his career, Sims played in Europe for five seasons, going to Austria, Switzerland, Germany and Scotland. He was 35 years old and wanted to retire and become a coach but needed a team willing to give him a chance. Instead, Komets coach Robbie Laird convinced him to play one more year by dangling an assistant coach's position. Sims scored seven goals and 37 points in 61 games.

"I think if you have the pride that you are an ex-NHL player, people expect certain things from you, and I always tried to live up to that," he said. "I loved playing the game, and it was the best time of my life, and when you go to a team that is lesser than the NHL, you want to show them that you have the work ethic and you still want to win at this level."

When Laird became an assistant coach with the Washington Capitals the next season in 1989, Sims became the Komets' new head coach. He was not an immediate success, going 37-34-0 and losing in the first round of the playoffs, but there was plenty of turmoil off the ice. Owner David Welker was battling the Memorial Coliseum board and eventually moved the team to Albany, N.Y., in the summer of 1990.

After the Franke brothers bought the defunct Flint Spirits and moved them to Fort Wayne as the new Komets, Sims orchestrated the rebirth of hockey in Fort Wayne. The Komets were a high-scoring, hard-hitting and always-fighting crew, though it took a little while for the city to realize how special they were. It wasn't until the Komets upset defending Turner Cup champion Indianapolis in the first round of the playoffs that Memorial Coliseum became "The Jungle."

The Komets lost in the Turner Cup Finals in 1991, but after a first-round upset in 1992, they swept all three series to win the title in 1993. It was a miracle run that shook the hockey world and earned Sims an interview to coach the expansion Anaheim Mighty Ducks. Sims didn't get the job, but he did get to move up as an assistant coach.

Did he think about staying in Fort Wayne to remain as a head coach?

"I did think about it, but my goal was always to get back to the NHL as a coach, and I thought that might be my stepping stone to being a head coach and getting some offers," Sims said. That's what happened after three years when Sims was hired to coach the San Jose Sharks in 1996-97. The Sharks had finished 20-55-7 the previous season, placing last in the Pacific Division.

General Manager Dean Lombardi built an older team with players such as Al Irafrate, Bernie Nichols, Tony Granato, Marty McSorley, Tim Hunter and Kelly Hrudey, but the Sharks were not much better, going 27-47-8.

"I had never lost as a coach, and it was a total failure," Sims said. "A lot of my friends saw me on the bench two-thirds or three-quarters of the way through the season, and they said, 'Christ, Al, what happened? You look like hell!' That's what losing does to you. It just wears on you."

Lombardi blamed Sims and fired him.

"He had player meetings with everybody before he had a meeting with me," Sims said. "He had an opinion formed by the older players. I wasn't a favorite of them because I couldn't get anything out of them. It came down to the players or me, and at that point, it's obviously better to change the coach than the players."

Sims signed to coach Milwaukee in the International Hockey League for three seasons, but he never got a chance to go back to the NHL.

"I think the problem was I jumped at an opportunity to go back to the minors because that's where I'd had success," he said. "I thought I needed to stay as a head coach to practice my trade. I didn't want to go back to being an assistant. I think that was a mistake, because if I had waited I probably would have gotten some assistant coaching offers, and maybe a head job interview. I didn't wait, and that might have been my fault that I didn't stay in the NHL longer."

He had decent success in Milwaukee over three seasons but could not get past the second round of the playoffs. He then spent five seasons in the Central Hockey League coaching Corpus Christi and Fort Worth before taking a job as general manager with Flint in 2006-07.

That's where he was when the Komets called in 2007 to ask if he'd be interested in coming back to Fort Wayne as coach. He jumped at the chance, and the Komets dominated the second coming of the IHL, winning three straight championships. After the IHL merged with the CHL in 2010, the Komets lost in the second round of the 2011 playoffs to Rapid City, but they came back in 2012 to win their fourth title in five years.

"There's no doubt I was a much better coach than the first time," Sims said. "The first couple of years, I was pretty much a wild man on the bench, yelling, screaming, pacing up and down and getting in guys' ears, yelling at referees across the ice."

Colin Chin, Komets captain in the '90s, tells the story about how he was sent by Sims over to talk to a referee one night.

"I know he's been calling you this and that all night, so just tell me anything and I'll go back and tell him we talked," Chin had said to the official. "I gotta look like I'm asking you what's going on, so don't get mad at me." Chin came back and said, "If you don't be quiet, he's going to give you a penalty."

"The one thing I really did (the second time as Komets coach) was I thought I was a lot calmer and knew that yelling all the time is not a good thing because people just turn you off, and players turn you off," Sims said. "I tried to pick my spots when I'd get angry or frustrated with the team, and it worked well in Fort Wayne."

It certainly helped to have spectacular team captains like Chin and Colin Chaulk. They carried Sims' message into the locker room and led the team on the ice.

After the Komets failed to make the playoffs in 2012-13, Sims' contract was not renewed. He took over at Evansville midseason in 2013-14, coaching the IceMen for two seasons before they went dormant.

Today, Sims coaches a prep school program in Toronto and loves it. But Fort Wayne will always be home.

"The playing part has to be the best part of my life, but the coaching success with Fort Wayne was some of the best years of my life," he said. "It was something I'll never forget. I'll always be a Komet and be available to help if they need something or an opinion on a player or whatever.

"Playing in the NHL was one thing, and coaching was totally different for me, but Fort Wayne to me was as close to the NHL as I could be because we were so good, so competitive and had a team that you were proud to coach. You tell them to try something and they would try it, just a great group of guys that went on for five years and really carried us to the championships. It's always the players that get it done, and I'm thankful for all the players I coached."

CHAPTER 24

Wiegmann provided home base for future stars

There will never be a Komets fan who has as much heart as Ruth Wiegmann, and she shares it with just about everyone.

While Ruth and Harold Wiegmann raised their family of four, they also (starting in 1964) hosted 78 foster children – all babies – and in 1983, they hosted their first of six foreign exchange students. In 1985, they started housing members of Fort Wayne's pro indoor soccer team, and in 1986, they started hosting members of the Komets.

Ever since, it seems there's always been at least one Komet staying at the Wiegmann house, more than 80 in all. Ruth Wiegmann became the Komets' unofficial "Mom," except the players often felt there was nothing unofficial at all.

Among the current or former Komets and future NHL players who have stayed at Ruth's house are Brad Aitken, Robin Bawa, Stephane Beauregard, Steve Maltais, Shawn Chambers, Stephan Brochu, Glenn Mulvenna, Ray LeBlanc, Frédéric Chabot, Kevin Kaminski and Eric Boguniecki. She's even got a Komets jersey with their numbers listed.

Players had to abide by Ruth's rules, but in return they had a free place to stay and free home-cooked meals; Wiegmann also washed all the laundry. They were all part of the family. Even players who have moved out regularly come back for dinner.

"Everybody has a purpose in life, and mine is to be a mother," she said. "You can give to missions and never know where it goes, but here we could see the results."

Every year, Wiegmann's Christmas card collection is huge, with letters coming from all over the world, and she continues to hear from many of the players' parents. She also has attended countless weddings.

At one time, there were five hockey players and four soccer players living in the house, and she once had 29 players and coaches come over for dinner as part of a team-bonding exercise. Then everyone played cards or board games.

Ruth Wiegmann and Colin Chaulk

Courtesy of The News-Sentinel

The funniest story Ruth tells involves Bawa. "Everybody had their place at the table, and one night, Robin switched with someone else. Everybody was laughing, but I had not caught on. He had had his ear pierced, and he sat on the other side where I wouldn't see it because he was worried what I'd say. He said (Steve Fletcher) made him do it."

Here was a 26-year-old man who regularly earned more than 300 penalty minutes and made it to the NHL who feared what a 4-foot-9 grandmother thought.

Guess he should have cleared it with Mom first.

CHAPTER 25

Icing the puck: odds and ends

99 ways a Komet made a great suggestion

When Wayne Gretzky joined the Ontario Hockey League's Sault Ste. Marie Greyhounds at age 16, he hoped to wear number 9 in honor of his favorite player, Detroit great Gordie Howe. Gretzky had always worn the number growing up, but unfortunately for him, the number was already being worn by the Greyhounds' Brian Gualazzi, meaning Gretzky had to come up with a new number.

Gretzky started by wearing number 19 and switched to 14. Then Greyhounds coach Murray "Muzz" MacPherson, a former Komets goaltender, remembered that when Phil Esposito had been traded from the Boston Bruins to the New York Rangers that season, he went from wearing number 7 to number 77 because number 7 belonged to the Rangers' Rod Gilbert.

"If you can't wear one number 9, wear two," MacPherson told Gretzky.

MacPherson later told the Ottawa Sun's Terry Jones, "Wayne was really worried that people would laugh at him if he wore number 99, but I convinced him to try it. They didn't laugh at him."

"At first, I said, 'No, that's too hot-doggish,'" Gretzky said. "But they convinced me to wear it."

Just before he died in 1997, MacPherson said, "If I don't give him that number, who knows who I am?"
He had a point. MacPherson played only twelve professional games, including three with the Komets in 1959-60. The thing MacPherson was most famous for was when the Komets loaned him to Troy for a game, and Fort Wayne lit him up in a 17-1 victory.

Wonder what it would get on eBay?

One of the most famous pucks in NHL Stanley Cup history is not sitting in the Hockey Hall of Fame in Toronto, and it's all a former Komet's fault.

Brett Hull scored the most controversial goal in finals history in 1999, when the Dallas Stars clinched the series by beating the Buffalo Sabres in overtime. While most of his teammates swarmed over Hull, defenseman Shawn Chambers grabbed the puck from behind Sabres goaltender Dominik Hasek and shoved it down his pants. Chambers had done the same thing a couple of years earlier as a member of the New Jersey Devils when they won the cup.

No one thought to ask where Hull's puck had disappeared to, and for several years, it sat on Chambers' television set before he moved it into a display case in his new home.

Not a trick of the eyes

Every once in a while, sharp-eyed fans of the comic "Hi and Lois" might spot a Komets pennant in the background on the wall in the comics character Ditto's room.

"Boy, people in Indiana sure have sharp eyes!" said artist Greg Walker, who works on the strip with his brother Brian and friend Robert "Chance" Browne. Greg and Brian are the sons of Mort Walker, and Chance is the son of Dik Browne, who originated the strip in 1954.

"A person on our staff currently lives in Indiana and likes to put references in the strip," Greg Walker wrote. "Every time he does, I get a bunch of e-mails."

The curse of the Komets

This one might be a minor league hockey version of an urban legend, but the facts make you wonder.

With a great team effort, the Komets tied Game 7 of the 1991 playoff s to force overtime against the Indianapolis Ice, the top farm club of the Chicago Blackhawks. During the intermission before the overtime, Chicago coach and General Manager Mike Keenan supposedly told the Ice players that if they lost, they'd never play for the Blackhawks. The Komets won 4-3 when Lonnie Loach slipped the puck between the pads of Indianapolis goaltender Jimmy Waite before defenseman Cam Russell could unload on him. While the Komets celebrated, the Ice players were crushed.

The Keenan story sounds suspicious until you consider what happened to the rest of those Ice players. Mike Stapleton, Dominik Hasek, Mike Eagles, Mike Peluso, Brian Noonan and Ryan McGill all had significant NHL careers – playing for teams other than the Blackhawks. Waite eventually played for Chicago, but only after first being traded to San Jose. Russell played for Chicago, but only after Keenan had been fired.

Perhaps Keenan's edict is what led to Chicago's 1992 trade of future NHL great Hasek to Buffalo for former Komet Stephane Beauregard.
Guess who just happened to be the winning goaltender in the 1991 overtime? Beauregard. Hasek became an all-time NHL great, while Beauregard never played a game for the Blackhawks.

With their farm system depleted, the Blackhawks struggled throughout the 1990s and goaltending in particular was always a problem.

NOTE: Though he later became an all-time NHL great, Dominik Hasek didn't dominate the Komets when he played for the Indianapolis Ice. Despite a 2.86 goals-against average, Hasek was 4-4-1 against Fort Wayne.

Pilling a few fast ones

For weeks, Saginaw had been gearing up to face Komets goaltender Murray Bannerman on March 24, 1978, but Komets coach Gregg Pilling pulled a few surprises.

Pilling started Robbie Irons in goal but sent Bannerman in with 17:43 left in the first period. Irons returned with 13:51 left only to be replaced by Bannerman with 10:42 left. Irons and Bannerman passed each other more often than ships in the night. The trend continued in the second period, with Bannerman going in with 17:06 left, followed by Irons at 7:30 and Bannerman at 4:39. During the third period, Bannerman came in at 14:27, and Pilling finished with Irons for the final eight seconds.

"Robbie started the game for us and he finished it for us," Pilling explained. "We had a heckofa lot of luck."

Everyone was waiting for Pilling to try changing goalies on the fly, but he said, "I've tried that before. It's a two-minute penalty." Combined, Irons made fourteen saves and Bannerman twenty-six as the Komets were outshot 40-20 but won 2-0 to stay in first place. There were nine goaltender switches in the game.

Bannerman later became a successful goalie with the Blackhawks before retiring in the Chicago area.

"That was my first year out of junior, and I remember Gregg Pilling was a little bit different than what I expected as a coach," Bannerman said in 1997. "He was a little more wide open to things."

Pilling later tried the same thing for the home fans against Toledo.

Instigating incident

The most remarkable statistic about Steve Fletcher isn't that he fought between 250 and 300 times during his pro career or that he earned almost 4,400 penalty minutes or even that he lasted 14 years at a job that burns most players out after five or six.

Steve Fletcher

Courtesy of The News Sentinel

It's that he earned only one instigation penalty throughout his career.

Oh, and he earned it.

Fletcher made his National Hockey League debut during a 1988 playoff game with the Montreal Canadiens against the Boston Bruins. The Canadiens had called up Fletcher from Sherbrooke of the American Hockey League to provide extra toughness. He ended up fighting the Bruins' Lyndon Byers.

"We were in a commercial break, and the next thing you know, his gloves were down and he was jumping on my back," Fletcher said. "I was bent over getting ready for the faceoff, not even paying attention. He never hit me in the face or hurt me because I was able to defend myself."

It took Fletcher five years to get Byers back. During the 1993-94 season, Fletcher challenged Byers to a fight before a faceoff in Las Vegas.

"He pretended he wasn't even paying attention, and then he jumped me again," Fletcher said. "I ended up winning the fight, but I wasn't happy because he tried to do the same thing again." So in Fort Wayne on March 9, 1994, Fletcher told Komets coach Bruce Boudreau what was going on, and Boudreau said, "Do whatever you have to."

Fletcher grabbed Byers from behind, swung him around and started throwing punches. Afterward in the penalty box, Byers said he couldn't believe Fletcher had jumped him. Fletcher couldn't believe Byers didn't remember and kept pointing to his back. In fact, Fletcher still thinks Byers was faking it again.

"I never wanted anybody to say I jumped them," Fletcher said. "I wanted a fair fight all the time, because I didn't want to hear any excuses after I beat you. I never ran; I stood up for whatever was coming."

Quick-draw Hrycuik

Jim Hrycuik liked fast starts. He scored the fastest goal in Komets history, taking a faceoff and scoring six seconds into a game against Muskegon on Jan. 31, 1973. He was a key midseason addition in Fort Wayne's 1973 Turner Cup run, scoring 12 goals in 21 games.

His career continued to move up thanks in part to NHL expansion. He joined the Washington Capitals in their inaugural

season, starting their first game on Oct. 9, 1974, against the New York Rangers in Madison Square Garden.
At 5:06 of the first period, Hrycuik came out of the corner with the puck and beat Hall of Fame goaltender Ed Giacomin to score the first goal in Capitals history.

Unfortunately, Hrycuik's career ended after 21 games that year because of a knee injury. He scored five goals and 12 points in his short NHL career.

A rookie to the rescue
Darren Jensen's first NHL game happened under the worst possible conditions.

When Philadelphia Flyers goaltender Pelle Lindbergh was killed in a car accident and his backup Bob Froese was injured in practice, the Flyers called up Jensen from Hershey of the American Hockey League to fill in on Nov. 14, 1985.

His opponents? Only the defending Stanley Cup champion Edmonton Oilers led by Wayne Gretzky, Mark Messier and Paul Coffey.

"It occurred to me," Jensen said, "that there might be easier teams to play against."

He made it look easy. After standing through a 23-minute pregame memorial service for Lindbergh, Jensen beat the Oilers 5-3, making 29 saves and holding Gretzky scoreless on seven shots.

"You tell yourself not to be awed by these guys, but it's hard," Jensen said.

Jensen played one season with the Komets in 1983-84 and made a lasting impression on the IHL by earning both the Rookie of the Year Award and the league Most Valuable Player Award. He signed with Philadelphia in 1984, playing 30 games over two seasons.

Tod Daleovich Hartje, Amerikanski

Tod Hartje was a hockey legend before he ever played a U.S. professional game.

Though it's a lot more common in today's hockey world, in 1990-91 Hartje became the first North American player ever to compete in the Soviet Elite League. He wrote the book From Behind the Red Line: An American Hockey Player in Russia detailing his experiences, including the use of a fake Soviet passport that said Tod Daleovich Hartje.

Published in 1992, the book became a hot seller in Fort Wayne and around the hockey world. Ironically, Hartje played as a Komet for one game at Peoria in December 1991 during his Christmas break from Russia and later in 1992-93 for five games.

The book was fascinating in its detail of the Russian life and hockey system. The biggest lesson Hartje learned is that people are people.

"I walked away convinced more than ever that Soviets are the same as you and I – people who just want to be accepted, people who have the same feelings and needs as we do," he wrote. "I allowed myself a corny thought – if we had gotten to know each other as people, instead of letting suspicion and prejudice prevail, the Cold War would never have happened."

Mark Wilkins
Courtesy of The News-Sentinel

Wilkins had close view of hockey's changes

Before he retired after 29 years, no one from Fort Wayne had a better view of the on-ice changes in hockey over the years than Mark Wilkins. As a lineman and referee, Wilkins called games in seven International Hockey League Turner Cup Finals, a Canada Cup, a World Championship, an NCAA Championship and 10 NCAA Regionals. He worked in every league below the National Hockey League, calling more than 2,000 games. He hung up his whistle after the 2014 Central Collegiate Hockey Association playoffs at age 48.

Over his last three years wearing the stripes, Wilkins estimated he'd driven more than 115,000 miles. During his career, he worked 15 years in the IHL and the last 14 in the CCHA.

"The speed of the game is much faster now," he said. "Players are stronger and faster. You see much more skill level at the ECHL and college level than you saw in the past. There's completely less physical play, more finesse. I don't think there's as much emphasis on physical play."

One of the highlights of his career was calling the 2010 Frozen Four championship game in Detroit. Boston College beat Wisconsin 5-0 as Wilkins worked his first Frozen Four game.

"Once the puck dropped, it was a normal game and it was `go' time," Wilkins said. "It was just make sure you make the right calls and see the play."

There were more than 37,000 people in Ford Field, including Wilkins' sons Kyle and Mitch and the game was also televised on ESPN.

"I'm usually anxious in the locker room before every game, but you know this has the potential to be the biggest college hockey game ever," Wilkins said. "I ordered my lunch, and I could barely get it down. Our supervisor said, `It's a big game, but it's just like any other game.' Then I loosened up and got into my usual routine."

Colligan helped start Notre Dame hockey legacy

When he went to his first Komets game at age 13, Stan Colligan fell in love with hockey because, as he said, there were a bunch of fights and everything else and it got into his blood. Partly because he couldn't skate well, Colligan became a goaltender, wearing his sister's figure skates, a catcher's chest protector, his baseball glove and no shoulder pads.

After graduating from Central Catholic in 1963, Colligan went to Notre Dame to study business. There was no hockey available, so a few buddies organized pick-up games on St. Mary'sLake by posting flyers in all the dorms. Notre Dame hockey started a club program in 1912 but ended in 1927.

The next season, Colligan and friends decided to get a little more organized and start an official club. There were four officers, and Colligan was the traveling secretary, which meant he set up the schedule and the travel arrangements. To pay for the ice time, they earned a nickel for each program they sold at the football games, and they charged $1 for showing movies in a school auditorium.

As a sophomore, Colligan quickly realized he wasn't a good enough goaltender so he tried out at right wing which lacked numbers. As a junior and senior he played defense for the same reason. The players wore white Notre Dame football jerseys as their uniforms.

The squad finished 6-6-3 during Colligan's senior year, and Notre Dame Athletic Director Moose Krause called a couple of the players to a meeting to ask for input on a new rink the school was building. After Colligan graduated with a finance degree in 1967, the first varsity hockey game was played in 1969.

Colligan, 72 and president of Colligan and Company Insurance Agency in 2017, attends one or two Notre Dame games a year, but he still startles his wife Cheryl sometimes with his yelling at the television screen while watching games. Now the Notre Dame hockey program is a perennial national power, and Colligan helped start it all.

Stan Colligan
Courtesy of The News-Sentinel

"You have to love it to play out there with some of those conditions," Colligan said. "We had each other and everybody loved the game."

CHAPTER 26

Essensa revitalized career in Fort Wayne

When Bob Essensa came back to the Komets in October 1995, he was a 30-year-old goaltender who was struggling so much that he had been basically booed out of Detroit.

He had been acquired by Detroit at the trade deadline from the Winnipeg Jets as supposedly the Red Wings' playoff savior in net, but he struggled down the stretch, going 4-7-2 late in the season and then getting beat 5-4 in the first game of the playoffs at home. The Red Wings lost to San Jose in five games, and their fans mostly blamed Essensa.

He spent the 1994-95 season playing with San Diego in the International Hockey League, going 6-8-1 with a 3.39 goals-against average. He could have retired, but the Red Wings had signed him to a three-year guaranteed contract worth $1.3 million annually. And Essensa was not a quitter.

Neither was Komets General Manager David Franke, who kept calling Detroit Assistant General Manager Dennis Holland to ask about Essensa. Five months after Franke started, Holland finally called in October to make the deal.

Most goaltenders being sent down need about three weeks to get over the funk, but Essensa was happy to come back to Fort Wayne, where he had played 22 games in 1988-89 as a Winnipeg Jets second-year pro, going 14-7-1.

"It was trying times for me personally and not an easy time, but it was a breath of fresh air to come down to Fort Wayne

Bob Essensa

Courtesy of The News-Sentinel

and enjoy playing again," Essensa said. "I got to be reunited with some of my college buddies, some of my Winnipeg Jets buddies and some guys who were there from my first stint in Fort Wayne."

He had played with Colin Chin, Carey Lucyk and assistant coach Derek Ray with the 1988-89 Komets; been roommates with Mitch Messier at Michigan State; and played with John LeBlanc, Ross Wilson, Shawn Cronin, Grant Richison, Andrew McBain and Pat Elynuik under coach Dave Farrish in Moncton, the Jets' American Hockey League farm club.

"They were all just very good, fun-loving guys," Essensa said. "You don't want to put too much stock in those types of teams, but most teams that find success find a way to have fun together. Quite honestly, that was one of the most enjoyable seasons I had as a pro because of the camaraderie I had with those guys."

Part of that fun was making jokes at Essensa's expense about his contract, which made him the highest-paid player in the minors that year and the highest-paid Komet ever. Chin and Messier used to joke around in the locker room by holding Essensa's pay envelope up to the light to see if they could tell what was written on his check.

"They told me as soon as I got down there that whenever we were playing card games in the back of the bus, I was never allowed to bluff," Essensa said with a laugh. "We used to have fun with it. If one of our buddies had a tough weekend, I'd hand them my (per diem) envelope and say, 'I'm buying for you, bud.' When it came to dinnertime, I was more than happy to pick up most of the tabs."

And Essensa was solid in the net. After regaining his confidence, he went on a 10-2-1 tear in the middle of the season and finished 24-14-5 to receive his teammates' Most Valuable Player vote. His regular season 2.89 goals-against average ranked third in the league and his .912 save percentage ranked second.

"He's the best goalie in the league," Komets captain Colin Chin said at the time. "Defense wins playoffs, and we know with Bob back there we can beat anybody."

Though Essensa was excellent in the first round with a 2.41 goals-against average and .923 save percentage, the Komets lost to Orlando 3-2 in a very good series. Everyone in the Fort

Wayne locker room felt the Komets had wasted some great goaltending and could have gone a long way if they had gotten past the Solar Bears.

"What was really tough about losing is that we squandered a chance to have that kind of goaltender in our lineup during the playoffs," Chin said. "We didn't do anything with Bob, and that's tough."

That summer, the Red Wings traded Essensa to Edmonton for future considerations. He played six more seasons in the NHL, never allowing more than 2.91 goals per game before retiring after the 2001-02 season.

"It was nice for me to get my footing again, and the guys in the locker room made it so easy," Essensa said. "I can't say enough about those guys. They made it fun to come to the rink, and it was a great refresher on what the game's all about and how fun it can be. I can't say enough about how coming to Fort Wayne helped me get myself back into the NHL."

CHAPTER 27

Knipscheer provided example for every local player

Fred Knipscheer
Courtesy of Boston Bruins

When Fred Knipscheer played high school hockey for Snider, he wasn't the biggest guy on the ice and he wasn't close to being the best. As a junior, he was a 5-foot-7, 145-pound defenseman. Despite helping the Panthers win two state titles, everyone told him he was too small for college hockey.

Seven years later, he was a 5-11, 187-pound center playing for the Boston Bruins in one of the most remarkable stories in Fort Wayne's hockey history. It probably never should have happened.

"I think I have more appreciation of what I accomplished now than I did back then," Knipscheer said from his home in Indianapolis. "When you are in the middle of it, you just go with the flow and try to play and have fun. What helped me a lot, too, was growing up in Fort Wayne, everyone dreams of playing pro sports, but I never thought it was attainable. I just wanted to play for the Komets. That was my lifetime goal."

Even then, it was an exceptionally tough goal to attain because Knipscheer didn't go to Michigan State or Wisconsin or Michigan or Miami of Ohio to play college hockey. He went to small St. Cloud State in Minnesota. There he became one of the leading scorers in Division I hockey with 34 goals and 26 assists over 36 games during his last season to earn second-team all-American honors.

When the Bruins signed him as a free agent in 1993, it was an astonishing ascent.

"It's actually a pretty weird experience," Knipscheer said after signing. "You look at these guys during warm-ups and it's like, 'Wow, I've been watching these guys for so long, and now I'm playing with them.' It was a shock at first, but once I got hit one time, I realized it was just another game."

After leading Providence of the American Hockey League with 26 goals and 39 points in 62 games, the Bruins called him up late in the year after Joe Juneau was traded, Cam Neely was knocked out for the rest of the season with an injury, and Ray Bourque suffered a season-ending knee injury. In his second NHL game, Knipscheer scored his first goal, the game-winner to help the Bruins beat Anaheim 5-3 on March 24, 1994.

"It was a perfect shuffle pass, and I one-timed it right between his legs," Knipscheer said. It happened so fast that, right when I shot it, I knew it was going in because it was wide open. It didn't hit me until after I turned. The crowd went nuts."

He played about 25 minutes, getting four shots on goal.

"During the first period, I think I was so excited that I was trying to do everything at the same time. I was skating 100 mph all the time, and I was exhausted after 20 seconds of each shift. In the locker room, I was telling myself to relax and slow down – let the game happen and not try to rush everything. I was a lot better in the second period. It helped knowing I was going to be out there every couple of minutes on a regular shift."

He scored three goals and five points in 11 games during the regular season and then two goals and three points in 12 playoff games. Even better, he scored the game-winning goal as the Bruins beat arch-rival Montreal in Game 7 of the playoffs. He still has the puck.

The next year, he started again in Providence, scoring 39 goals and 63 points in 71 games before being called up on March 21. Then he scored three goals in his first three games with the Bruins before suffering a dislocated right shoulder.

During training camp in 1995, the Bruins shocked Knipscheer by trading him to St. Louis for defenseman Rick Zombo. He finished his Boston career with 43 games, eight goals and 12 points.

He got one game with the Blues but spent the year in the AHL with Worcester, scoring 36 goals and 73 points in 68 games.

After that season, he bounced around the minors to play in Phoenix, Indianapolis, Utah, Kentucky, Cincinnati and Milwaukee before three concussions in three months forced him to retire in 2000.

"The things I've done are 1,000 times more than I could have ever imagined doing in hockey," he said. "The last couple of weeks, I've just spent time going over some of those things. I can tell my kids some great stories."

Today, Knipscheer owns a restaurant in Indianapolis where he's been a youth coach for years.

"Like I tell all the kids that I coach, it doesn't matter where you start or where you come from or at what age you mature, if you have a dream, follow it and give it everything you have," he said. "If you are good enough and lucky enough to get a few breaks, you can make it to the highest level. I'm living proof of that."

He might have been able to accomplish even more except for the concussions. Knipscheer estimated that between high school football, college hockey and pro hockey, he suffered 12. Only one came from a cheap hit, causing the dislocated shoulder in Boston, but the rest were because of circumstances. One time he hit his head on the glass when he was being checked. Another time he got flipped into the air and landed on his head. Another time he was skating up to check someone and they reflexively reacted by turning their shoulder and hitting Knipscheer in the jaw.

Those injuries affected the way Knipscheer coaches. When he was coaching 6 and 7-year-olds, he started with contact drills.

"I've always been a big believer that even though the game chanced a lot, you can't play with fear or without contact. You just can't, so I've always tried to teach how to deal with contact and how to handle it. I had parents ask me why I was doing it so early, and I said these kids have to learn that hockey is a contact sport, and the sooner they learn it, the less fear they will have when checking is allowed. We worked on it for three years, and when our kids became pee wees, the fear was gone. They learned how to do it effectively and receive a hit as well. I think my kids had two concussions in the eight years I coached them.

I think the way we coached had a lot to do with that."

Now with all the news about how concussions are affecting former athletes, Knipscheer said he's glad he got out when he did without further damage. "My family likes to give me grief when I don't remember everything, but I do have documentation." He's happy and fulfilled in his life. Other than being sore every morning, Knipscheer has only one regret, that he never got to play for his hometown team.

"More so because of my parents and friends and family in Fort Wayne who supported me," he said. "If I wouldn't have gotten hurt, I believe I would have played for them at least a year or two, because that was something I always wanted to do. I was 31 when I retired, and I planned on playing until I was much older than that. That's my biggest disappointment and regret."

But the way he played and the fact that he played in the NHL proved an inspiration for many other Fort Wayne players. Before Knipscheer, coaches said it was possible to play in the NHL only if everything went exactly right. Most things didn't go right for Knipscheer, but he still achieved his dream.

"It's a cool thing to have kids look up to you and follow in your footsteps, and maybe they can fulfill their dream. I tell kids all the time that I coach in Indy, 'If you work hard enough and if you are good enough, you'll get an opportunity, and it doesn't matter where you come from.

"Now that I am older and get a chance to look back at it, I'm proud of what I accomplished, and it's pretty cool."

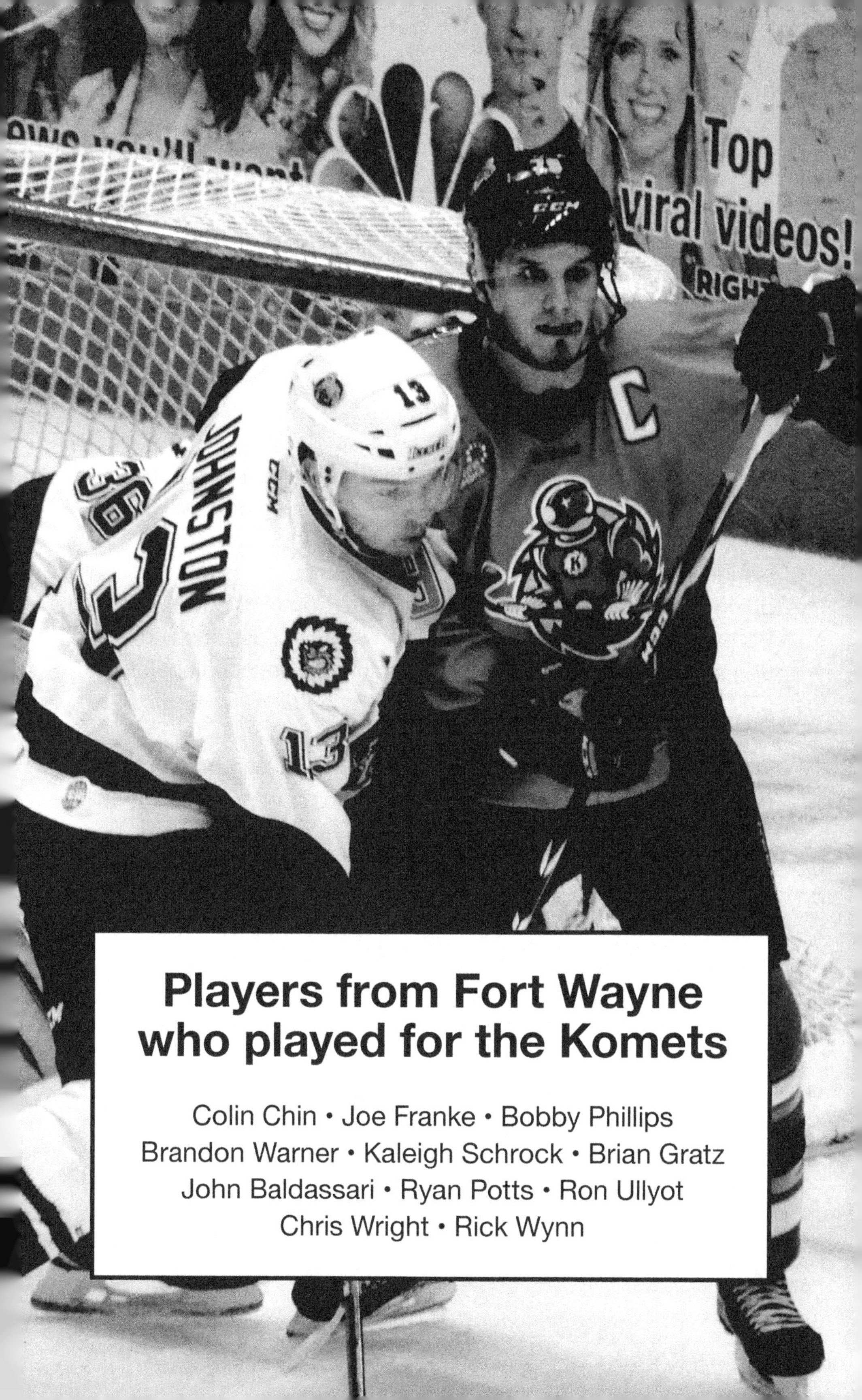

Players from Fort Wayne who played for the Komets

Colin Chin • Joe Franke • Bobby Phillips
Brandon Warner • Kaleigh Schrock • Brian Gratz
John Baldassari • Ryan Potts • Ron Ullyot
Chris Wright • Rick Wynn

CHAPTER 28

Purinton still fighting to change hockey

Dale Purinton wants everyone to know he doesn't hate hockey. In fact, he will always love the game.

He just hates what the sport did to him.

Purinton, the first Fort Wayne-born NHL player, has joined more than 100 former players suing the league about concussions. No, they don't want any money individually; they want the league to invest in research about what concussions are doing to current and former players. NHL Commissioner Gary Bettman has denied there's a link between concussions and the degenerative brain disease chronic traumatic encephalopathy (CTE).

The NFL gets so much credit for donating to research, Purinton said, but people forget they were forced to do that.

"I'm not here to bash hockey or the NHL," Purinton said from his home in Duncan, British Columbia. "I'm not trying to hurt the game, I'm trying to make it better. I have three kids who play hockey, and they love hockey and I love hockey. I owe a lot to the game, but there's a lot of stuff that can be changed, and if it starts there, we can protect someone else from going through what I have."

And that's been a great deal because Purinton almost ended up in prison for life. He blames concussions for the majority of his problems.

Dale Purinton
Courtesy of New York Rangers

Because his father, Cal, was a stalwart defenseman for the Komets and won two Turner Cups, Dale was born in Fort Wayne in 1976 and lived there until he was 4 years old when the family moved to Sicamous, British Columbia. His brother Terry still lives in Fort Wayne with his son Owen.

After playing junior hockey in Lethbridge, Alberta, Dale was drafted by the New York Rangers in the fifth round of the 1995 entry draft. The defenseman was big, tough and dependable, making it to the Rangers to play 181 games over five seasons.

"It's better than any dream you can imagine," his father said when Dale was called up for his first game in 2000. "It's one of those things I wish every parent could experience. I'm so proud of him it isn't even funny. You always dream and hope your kid will make it, in anything. It's not only my dream, but it's his. This is his dream, too."

Dale Purinton's statistics included 578 penalty minutes, four goals and 20 points – and also multiple concussions. He believes his first one happened when he was 17 and playing in juniors. He guesses he suffered at least 10 concussions while playing the game, though he never went through concussion protocol, which is required today. His last was March 30, 2004, when he was accidentally kicked in the chin with a skate by Jamie Langenbrunner.

"Most of the times, I just wouldn't talk about them or tell my teammates because you lose your job that way," he said. "There were times in juniors when I had them and didn't even know what they were."

After the skate to the chin, Purinton said that within two weeks, the season was over and he was cleared medically to go home. As the league went through a lockout in 2004-05, he battled nausea, headaches, depression, suicidal thoughts and forgetfulness. He also underwent personality changes. But talking about injuries was a sign of weakness, he'd been taught.

"I don't know if I was ever really the same after that," he said. "The problems got worse and worse, (as did) the self-medicating. There was a time when I never thought there was a way out of this. I was by myself and embarrassed."

Purinton played three more seasons in the minors before retiring at the end of the 2007-08 season. He admits he was an alcoholic and an addict, in part to deal with social anxiety.

"You don't even want to be there, something that you've done your whole life, and your family was a hockey family way before you were even born," he said. "I grew up in the rinks, and then I didn't even want to go near one."

Then he got in real trouble.

During the summer of 2015, Purinton was arrested for assault and burglary when he broke into the home of an acquaintance. With the encouragement of his wife, Temple, Purinton checked into Cedars at Cobble Hill, a residential addiction treatment center.

"When I fought that guy, he almost died, and I was pretty close to going away for the rest of my life," Purinton said. "That was the wake-up call that something wasn't right. To try to deal with all of my stuff with drugs and alcohol ... What's the underlying issue, and why at one time was everything fine and your decisions and life were good and you were happy and you didn't have depression and anxiety? It all led back to the same thing.

"I knew I was either going to end up dead or in jail the rest of my life, or I had to work on myself and deal with these issues."

After his treatment, Purinton served six months in prison, which he said gave him more opportunity to reflect and study. He used the chance to talk with others and try to help them and learn more about himself. Now he's been sober for more than two years, working as a logger. He loves spending time with his family, especially going to watch his three boys play. He's involved with a 12-step program and offers to help counsel others.

"Our lives have totally changed, almost like it wasn't real, but you can't get complacent," he said. "When you do, you know what happens. You always try to keep it at arm's length without being shameful or feeling guilty. You wonder why you had those experiences, and maybe it's not always a negative thing. It was tough and very bad, but how can we turn it around and make it an amazing thing?"

So now he's speaking out against NHL practices in hopes that it saves others from going through what he did. He doesn't want the league to end fighting, saying he figures maybe 20 percent of concussions come during fights, but what about the other 80 percent? He swears he's not trying to hurt the game but make it better for his sons and everyone else's sons who want to play. He gets asked all the time why he lets his sons play hockey if he knows the type of things that happened to him can still happen.

"I love hockey and they love hockey," he said. "I just want it to be safer. The game itself is amazing, the rules just need changed. It's just baffling that they are trying to deny this when scientifically it's proven. Just take care of the players! We want money put toward medical research and monitoring so we can help these guys so they are not suicidal or stuck in their home and don't go through life depressed. These are common things for guys who played the game.

"I love the game, but I think they are doing a poor job by not changing some of these rules. They have an opportunity here. (Commissioner) Bettman's legacy could be that he made the NHL a lot of money but he also made the game safer for kids."

The way Purinton looks at his life, he's one of the lucky ones, unlike Bob Probert, John Kordic, Rick Rypien, Derek Boogaard, Wade Belak and Steve Montador who all died from dealing with issues related to concussions.

"All these guys were warriors and battled hard for their team, and then they just discarded them when they had problems and called them drug addicts and alcoholics," Purinton said. "But what's the underlying issue? It's about the NHL, but also guys playing in the minors and college and juniors, because the younger leagues follow the NHL's lead.

"I'll continue to fight for guys and their rights, for people who are struggling. One day, I'd love to see all this come to the forefront and guys get taken care of once they are done playing. I'll be happy if that happens."

CHAPTER 29

Kaminski helped set up decades of Komets success

Kevin Kaminski
Courtesy of Washington Capitals

Of all the things the Fort Wayne Komets have accomplished over the last three decades, including six championships, there's a good chance none of it would have happened without Kevin Kaminski.

Though he only played one season in Fort Wayne, scoring nine goals and 24 points along with earning 455 penalty minutes, Kaminski set up the key goal that set up the modern Komets franchise.

On April 21, 1991, in Game 7 of a first-round playoff series against the defending Turner Cup champion Indianapolis Ice, Kaminski was carrying the puck inside the Komets' zone when he spotted winger Lonnie Loach cutting across the Indianapolis blue line all alone. Kaminski flipped a backhand saucer pass that landed on the tape of Loach's stick, and he split the Ice defensemen before cutting in on goaltender Jimmy Waite. Loach pushed the puck between Waite's pads to end the overtime game at 18:29 and quiet the Fairgrounds Coliseum crowd.

"We spent every last penny we had in that game," Kaminski said. "I didn't even want to get out of my equipment because we were so tired, just spent. If we don't win that game, then all those other things don't happen, so many great moments from that year."

Without that goal, the Komets wouldn't have won an epic series in the next round against division-champion Kalamazoo and advanced to the finals where the "(John) Anderson Game" happened, after which Bruce Boudreau followed with another miracle. That season set up the Franke Brothers' ownership for the next quarter century.

The season also set up Kaminski's career, and he went on to play 137 games in the NHL with the Washington Capitals. He also won a Calder Cup in the AHL with Portland.

But the way he played took a toll on his body. Kaminski cracked almost every bone in his body at one time or another and was laced back up with more than 650 stitches. After he was hit by a slap shot in 1998, he lost some vision in one eye and had two steel plates and 12 screws implanted in his face. He can't lay on either side to sleep because of his shoulders. He retired in 2000 at age 31 to start his coaching career.

Kaminski also estimates he's received at least 18 concussions. The legend of Killer Kaminski wasn't that he fought all the time or that he beat up a lot of guys. It was that he always somehow got back up and was ready to go again.

"I never shut my mouth, and I was always yapping," he said. "If I was 6 foot 4, I probably wouldn't have gotten into those fights. Who's going to want to fight a 6-4 guy who is trying to stir things up? If you're smart, you'll skate away. They look at a 5-9 guy and think, 'Heck, I can handle him.' I think that's when

I instigated that part and people would finally get ticked off because I was nagging in your side, I was a pain in the butt, and I'm going to get you to fight one way or another."

Late in the 1990-91 season, Kaminski's face was so built up with scar tissue that someone could flick him around the eyes with a finger and he'd start bleeding. A former teammate gave him the nickname "Paper Face."

By today's rules, Kaminski would have earned more than 750 penalty minutes that season, if he was allowed to play around suspensions. Many of his fights started because he jumped opponents from behind, and he was always quick to jump in when another tilt was already started.

"I probably lost more fights than I won," he said. "I love pain, I just love it. I'm in a lot of pain, my whole body, but I've had so many compliments from people asking how I just kept getting back up. When I put the skates on, I become a different breed. There's something inside of me that I'm willing to do whatever it takes for my teammates, to sacrifice my body, blocking shots, or taking the hit to make a play or getting punched in the face, all those things. Being kind of vulnerable ... that's kind of the way it was.

"I think it's contagious. This guy is 5-9, and if he's doing whatever it takes, your teammates might become a little braver and do the same thing."

The truly scary part was that Kaminski weighed only 170 pounds. He always had trouble putting on weight, and that meant he was always, always fighting opponents who were at minimum three inches and 30 pounds heavier. Fans used to cringe as much as cheer when watching him go toe-to-toe with the heavyweights.

"That's the way I grew up, I just hated to lose," he said. "I loved to win, and I'd do anything to get the W. That wasn't just in hockey, that was in ball and playing street hockey, that was anything I did. I think it was born in me. I would get ticked off losing a game of cards or whatever it was. It showed in the way I played. I needed to win."

That's kind of how he made his spot on the Komets. After fracturing his sternum and blowing his shoulder out in training camp in 1989, Kaminski played only 19 games in Halifax that season. He played seven games to start 1990-91 when he was sent to Fort Wayne.

And then coach Al Sims gave him a chance. During a game in Muskegon, Kamsinki challenged Lumberjacks' enforcer Mitch Wilson.

"Obviously, I had a great fight," Kaminski said. "Everybody on the bench thought I was crazy. Even Bruce Boudreau said, 'We all thought you were going to get your butt kicked. You don't look like a tough guy.' It showed them that maybe this kid was for real."

The Komets already had plenty of scoring with Boudreau, Anderson and Loach on one line, Colin Chin, Bob Lakso and then Scott Gruhl. That left Kaminski to mainly play with Robin Bawa and Steve Fletcher on the third line, though sometimes with Bruce Major, Ian Boyce or Peter Hankinson filling in. Bawa earned 381 penalty minutes and Fletcher 289 that season, mostly playing against opponents' top lines.

On the opening faceoff, opponents would look across at the "Ice Patrol" line and say, "You guys aren't going to be out here all night are you?" Fletcher loved to say, "Every shift."

"It was good to have some size on your line," Kaminski said. "I didn't go out there to flaunt it or say I was tough, but I knew deep inside I was tough and I could hold my own. When you get Fletch and Bawa on my line ... I'm 5-9, but I want to play like I'm 6-2, but with those guys I played like I was 6-5. I ran around and chirped a little bit more to get the other team off their game when I knew I had that support on the ice."

Going hard every shift is the way Kaminski coaches today as he leads the Fresno Monsters of the Western States Hockey League, a junior league that plays mostly in the cities of the former West Coast Hockey League.

"I tell them that I've been through the trenches, and I know what it takes to get there, so let me help you," he said. "Your individual accolades are important, too, but you have to do things for the team first. I tell the leading scorer, 'You have to do the same things as the third- and fourth-line guys, block shots or setting up plays. You have to to be a 200-foot player, not just a one-dimensional player.'"

He's trying to teach them to play with everything they have so they have no regrets later. Kaminski doesn't, because he gave everything he had to the game.

"Oh, there are some days I wish I would have used my skill a little bit more," he said with a chuckle. "There are times when my whole body is really, really sore, and I wish I wouldn't have done that, but you know what? No, to be able to play in the top six (top two lines) in the NHL, you have to be a very special player. I had good skill and vision, but was I a top-six forward? Would I have stuck around as a top-six forward?

"I accepted my role and chipped in whenever I could, and it lasted four years. If I tried another way, would it have lasted as long? I don't know."

CHAPTER 30

Being called No. 1 is not always great

There have been 17 first-round NHL draft picks who have played for the Fort Wayne Komets over the years, but sometimes that's not very good news for the players. Usually, it has meant they are on the downside of their careers and things haven't worked out the way they dreamed.

"It's not worth bragging rights or anything," Edmonton Oilers 1993 top pick Nick Stajduhar said in 2000. "It hasn't done me any favors, because it puts more pressure on you. Once you get drafted, it doesn't matter because guys in the 12th or 13th round go to camp and have the same chance as you."

The NHL amateur draft started in 1963 when there were only six NHL teams, and it was changed to an entry draft in 1979.

There have been a couple of No. 1 overall draft picks who have played for Fort Wayne. Rick Pagnutti was the first overall selection by Montreal in 1967. He played 121 games with the Komets in 1970-71 and 1971-72. He had a nine-year career in the minors but never made it to the NHL.

Doug Wickenheiser had the opposite situation. He was selected No. 1 overall by Montreal in 1980 and started immediately with the Canadiens. He played 10 years in the NHL with Montreal, St. Louis, Vancouver, the New York Rangers and Washington. He was a solid NHL player, but a knee injury in 1985 with St. Louis ruined any chance for greatness. He finished with 111 goals and 276 points in 556 career NHL games.

Mario Larocque
Courtesy of The News-Sentinel

Wickenheiser finished his pro career by playing 73 games with the Komets in 1993-94, scoring 22 goals and 59 points in 73 games. That summer, it was discovered that Wickenheiser was suffering from a rare form of cancer. He lost his battle on Jan. 12, 1999, at age 37.

From 1987 to 1994, the NHL also held supplemental drafts for players who had graduated from college hockey. Eventual Komets who were first-round picks in supplemental drafts include Rob Doyle, Brian McKee, Mike Natyshak, Mike DeCarle, Shawn Chambers, Phil Berger, Mike McNeill, Mike O'Neill, Doug Melnyk, Peter Hankinson, Ian Boyce, Craig Charron, Mark Richards, Jeff McLean, Dan Gravelle, Richard Shulmistra and Chad Dameworth.

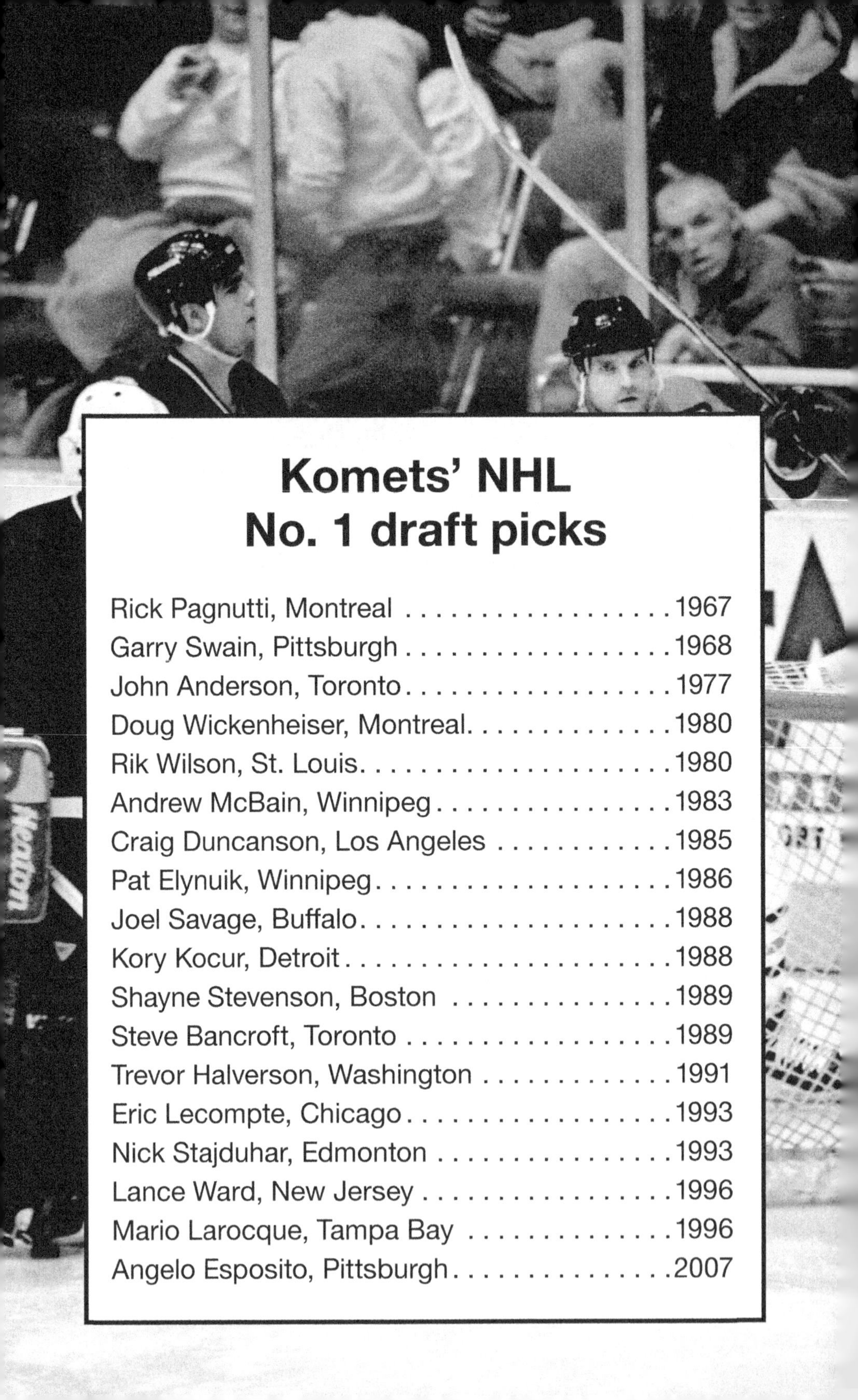

Komets' NHL No. 1 draft picks

Player, Team	Year
Rick Pagnutti, Montreal	1967
Garry Swain, Pittsburgh	1968
John Anderson, Toronto	1977
Doug Wickenheiser, Montreal	1980
Rik Wilson, St. Louis	1980
Andrew McBain, Winnipeg	1983
Craig Duncanson, Los Angeles	1985
Pat Elynuik, Winnipeg	1986
Joel Savage, Buffalo	1988
Kory Kocur, Detroit	1988
Shayne Stevenson, Boston	1989
Steve Bancroft, Toronto	1989
Trevor Halverson, Washington	1991
Eric Lecompte, Chicago	1993
Nick Stajduhar, Edmonton	1993
Lance Ward, New Jersey	1996
Mario Larocque, Tampa Bay	1996
Angelo Esposito, Pittsburgh	2007

CHAPTER 31

A treasured memento, Fort Wayne detective gave back a Komets jersey

Before every Komets game he attended over 15 years, Joe Lyon would pull on the same game-worn jersey that he'd paid $300 for at the 1993-94 postseason fan party. At the end of each season, he'd take it off, fold it carefully and place it in a box for storage.

But one time, he put the jersey in a box for a different reason: to send it home where it belongs.

On March 27, 2008, as the Komets were beating Flint 2-0, Lyon, a detective with the Fort Wayne Police Department, stood up to let his wife and daughter out of their row during an intermission. They usually sit in the lower arena, but for some reason on this night, their tickets were in the upper deck. When Lyon stood, Randy Marcom looked over from his upper-deck position as the broadcaster for the Public Access "Game of the Week" and saw the jersey Lyon was wearing – the last one Doug Wickenheiser ever wore in a pro game.

"At the time, I knew I wasn't going to get any of the big names, but I wanted a jersey," Lyon said. "I focused in on Wick's because he was such a calm presence on the ice. It always seemed when they did some boneheaded move on the ice, they'd send Doug out and everybody calmed down, and they got back to what they were supposed to be doing."

A true gentleman on and off the ice, Wickenheiser was known during his career for being the No. 1 overall pick in the 1980 draft by the Montreal Canadiens and for coming back from an injury that shredded all his left knee ligaments in the summer of 1985.

It had happened during a night off in 1985. Wickenheiser and some friends were goofing around when he jumped off the back of a truck, slipped, fell backward and was hit by a car. The ligaments in his left knee were shredded, and doctors told him he would never play again. They advised him to quit.

He came back within nine months. During the sixth game of the Campbell Conference finals against Calgary in 1986, he scored the game-winning goal in overtime. "The Monday Night Miracle" made Wickenheiser a legend in St. Louis.

"I guess because of the nature of the surgery, there were some doubts, but I never doubted it," Wickenheiser said in 1993. "I've never really felt anything noticeable with it. After I came back, some people said they noticed I was skating slower. Some people said they didn't notice any difference. I don't even worry about it."

After leaving St. Louis in 1987, Wickenheiser bounced around the NHL, the minors and Europe. He played 597 games in 10 NHL seasons, the last with the Washington Capitals during 1989-90. After playing a year in Italy and a season in Austria, Wickenheiser played with the Peoria Rivermen in 1992-93 before finishing up with the 1993-94 Komets, scoring 22 goals and 59 points in 73 games and helping lead the team back to the Turner Cup Finals. Then he went home to St. Louis.

Shortly after leaving Fort Wayne, a tumor was discovered in Wickenheiser's wrist. Eventually, the cancer spread to his throat

Doug Wickenheiser
Courtesy of The News-Sentinel

and into his brain. He died in 1999 at age 37, survived by his wife, Dianne, and daughters Rachel, Kaitlyn and Carly.

"He's a very honest, very loyal and very classy guy," said former Komets teammate Mitch Messier who visited Wickenheiser shortly before he passed away. "That's the biggest thing I can say. He wasn't too good for anybody. He always made time."

Marcom visited Wickenheiser a few months before he died. He had been good friends with Wickenheiser's brother Claude since he came to Fort Wayne to play senior hockey in 1973.

"One afternoon before a game, Claude mentioned, 'Yeah, my little brother should someday play in the NHL,'" Marcom said. "In so many words, I told him he was crazy, but five years later, he was the No. 1 overall draft choice."

After Marcom tapped him on the shoulder, Lyon told the story of the jersey and how he had always wanted to send it to Wickenheiser's family. Marcom helped him call Claude.

"Claude said he'd be willing to buy it from me, but I told him, 'I'm not charging you for your brother's jersey,'" Lyon said.

Except for a few puck marks, the jersey is in perfect condition, complete with the 1994 International Hockey League All-Star Game patch and the tie-down strap on the inside. The only thing added is Wickenheiser's signature from that postseason party.

Claude Wickenheiser was surprised by Lyon's call and the gesture.

"It's pretty touching," he said. "I'm sure the jersey meant a lot to him, too, but he just said it belongs to the family. That says there's a special quality about the man that he would do something like this."

The ironic thing is that of all the memorabilia Doug gave him over the years, Claude donated almost all of it to charities or special events. He had hardly anything left – and not one jersey.

"It belongs with the family," Lyon said. "It doesn't need to be haunting the coliseum. It's finally going to the right place."

CHAPTER 32

Komets in the NHL

NHL players who later played for the Komets

NHL teams, years in the NHL

Peter Ambroziak: Buffalo, 1994-95

John Anderson: Toronto, Quebec, Hartford, 1977-78 thru 1988-89

Bob Attwell: Colorado, 1979-80 thru 1980-81

Steve Bancroft: Chicago, 1992-93

Ralph Barahona: Boston, 1990-91 thru 1991-92

Bill Bennett: Boston, Hartford, 1978-79 thru 1979-80

Marc Boileau: Detroit, 1961-62

Bruce Boudreau: Toronto, Chicago, 1976-77 thru 1985-86

Stephan Brochu: New York Rangers, 1988-89

Paul Broten: New York Rangers, Dallas, St. Louis, 1989-90 thru 1995-96

Eric Calder: Washington, 1981-82 thru 1982-83

Tony Camazzola: Washington, 1981-82

Luca Caputi: Pittsburgh, Toronto, 2009-10 thru 2010-11

Stephane Charbonneau: Quebec, 1991-92

Dave Chartier: Winnipeg, 1980-81

Tim Cheveldae: Detroit, Winnipeg, Boston, 1990-91 thru 1996-97

Chris Clifford: Chicago, 1984-85 thru 1988-89

Sylvain Couturier: Los Angeles, 1988-89 thru 1991-92

Shawn Cronin: Washington, Philadelphia, San Jose, 1988-89 thru 1994-95

Dan Currie: Edmonton, Los Angeles, 1990-91 thru 1993-94

Marc D'Amour: Calgary, Philadelphia, 1985-86 thru 1988-89

P.C. Drouin: Boston, 1996-97

Parris Duffus: Phoenix, 1996-97

Craig Duncanson: Los Angeles, Winnipeg, New York Rangers, 1988-89 thru 1992-93

Corey Elkins: Los Angeles, 2009-10

Pat Elynuik: Washington, Winnipeg, Tampa Bay, Ottawa, 1987-88 thru 1995-96

Shawn Evans: St. Louis, New York Islanders, 1985-86 thru 1989-90

Trevor Fahey: New York Rangers, 1964-65

Todd Flichel: Winnipeg, 1987-88 thru 1989-90

Pierre Gagne: Boston, 1959-60

Dave Gagnon: Detroit, 1990-91

Daniel Goneau: New York Rangers, 1996-97 thru 1999-2000

David Goverde: Los Angeles, 1991-92 thru 1993-94

Brent Gretzky: Tampa Bay, 1993-94 thru 1994-95

Scott Gruhl: Los Angeles, Pittsburgh, 1981-82 thru 1987-88

Radek Hamr: Ottawa, 1992-93 thru 1993-94

Jeff Harding: Pittsburgh, 1988-89 thru 1989-90

Todd Harkins: Calgary, Hartford, 1991-92 thru 1993-94

Mark Holden: Montreal, Winnipeg, 1980-81 thru 1984-85

Doug Horbul: Kansas City, 1974-75

Todd Hrynewich: Pittsburgh, 1982-83 thru 1983-84

Peter Ing: Toronto, Edmonton, Detroit, 1989-90 thru 1993-94

Darren Jensen: Philadelphia, 1984-85 thru 1985-86

David Jensen: Hartford, Washington, 1983-84 thru 1987-88

Paul Jerrard: Minnesota, 1988-89

Jay Johnston: Washington, 1980-81 thru 1981-82

Brad Jones: Winnipeg, Los Angeles, Philadelphia, 1986-87 thru 1991-92

Les Kunter: Montreal, 1993-94

Jean-Marc Lanthier: Vancouver, 1983-84 thru 1987-88

Mario Larocque: Tampa Bay, 1998-99

John LeBlanc: Vancouver, Edmonton, Winnipeg, 1986-87 thru 1994-95

Craig Levie: Winnipeg, Minnesota, Vancouver, St. Louis, 1981-82 thru 1986-87

Hector Marini: New Jersey, New York Islanders, 1978-79 thru 1983-84

Bob Mason: Washington, Quebec, Vancouver, Chicago, 1983-84 thru 1990-91

Andrew McBain: Winnipeg, Pittsburgh, Vancouver, Ottawa, 1983-84 thru 1993-94

Doug McCaig: Detroit, Chicago, 1941-42 thru 1950-51

Jeff McLean: San Jose, 1993-94

Chris McRae: Toronto, Detroit, 1987-88 thru 1989-90

Mitch Messier: Minnesota, 1987-88 thru 1990-91

Oleg Mikulchik: Winnipeg, Anaheim, 1993-94 thru 1995-96

Kevin Miehm: St. Louis, 1992-93 thru 1993-94

Carl Mokosak: Calgary, Los Angeles, Philadelphia, Pittsburgh, Boston, 1981-82 thru 1988-89

Rob Murphy: Vancouver, Ottawa, Los Angeles, 1987-88 thru 1993-94

Mike Natyshak: Quebec, 1987-88

Greg Naumenko: Anaheim, 2000-01

Roman Oksiuta: Edmonton, Vancouver, Anaheim, Pittsburgh, 1993-94 thru 1996-97

Bill Oleschuk: Kansas City, Colorado, 1975-76 thru 1979-80

Dave Parro: Washington, 1980-81 thru 1983-84

Tom Pederson: San Jose, Toronto, 1991-92 thru 1996-97

Cam Plante: Toronto, 1984-85

Paul Pooley: Winnipeg, 1984-85 thru 1985-86

John Purves: Washington, 1990-91

Bruce Racine: St. Louis, 1995-96

Jean-Marc Richard: Quebec, 1987-88 thru 1989-90

Gerry Rioux: Winnipeg, 1982-83

Jeff Rohlicek: Vancouver, 1987-88 thru 1988-89

Joel Savage: Buffalo, 1990-91

Scott Shaunessy, Quebec 1986-87 thru 1988-89

Jim Shires: Detroit, St. Louis, Pittsburgh, 1971-71 thru 1972-73

Ron Shudra: Edmonton, 1987-88

Al Sims: Boston, Hartford, Los Angeles, 1973-74 thru 1982-83

Rick St. Croix: Philadelphia, Toronto, 1977-78 thru 1984-85

Nick Stajduhar: Edmonton, 1995-96

Shayne Stevenson: Boston, Tampa Bay, 1990-91 thru 1992-93

Garry Swain: Pittsburgh, 1968-69

Glen Tomalty: Winnipeg, 1979-80

Kirk Tomlinson: Minnesota, 1987-88

Mike Torchia: Dallas, 1994-95

Doug Wickenheiser: Montreal, St. Louis, New York Rangers, Washington, 1980-81 thru 1989-90

Rik Wilson: St. Louis, Calgary, Chicago, 1981-82 thru 1987-88

Chris Winnes: Boston, Philadelphia, 1990-91 thru 1993-94

Kevin Wortman: Calgary, 1993-94

Komets who later played in the NHL

NHL teams, years in the NHL, games played in NHL

Brad Aitken: Pittsburgh, Edmonton, 1987-88 thru 1990-91, 9 games (14 overall)

Chris Armstrong: Minnesota, Anaheim, 2000-01 thru 2003-04, 7 games

Darren Banks: Boston, 1992-93 thru 1993-94, 20 games

Murray Bannerman: Vancouver, Chicago, 1977-78 thru 1986-87, 289 games

Andrei Bashkirov: Montreal, 1998-99 thru 2000-01, 30 games

Robin Bawa: Washington, Vancouver, San Jose, Anaheim, 1989-90 thru 1993-94, 61 games

Stephane Beauregard: Winnipeg, Philadelphia, 1989-90 thru 1993-94, 90 games

Tim Bergland: Washington, Tampa Bay, 1989-90 thru 1993-94, 182 games

Les Binkley: Pittsburgh, 1968-69 thru 1971-72, 196 games, 81 WHA

John Blue: Boston, Buffalo, 1992-93 thru 1995-96, 5 games (41 overall)

Eric Boguniecki: Florida, St. Louis, Pittsburgh, New York Islanders, 1999-2000 thru 2006-07, 178 games

Mike Boland: Kansas City, Buffalo, 1974-75 thru 1978-79, 22 games (23 overall)

Dan Bonar: Los Angeles, 1980-81 thru 1982-83, 170 games

Eric Bolton: Buffalo, Atlanta, New Jersey, New York Islanders, 2000-01 thru 2015-16, 654 games

Viacheslav Butsayev: Philadelphia, San Jose, Anaheim, Florida, Ottawa, Tampa Bay, 1992-93 thru 1999-2000, 8 games (132 games overall)

Dave Cameron: Colorado, New Jersey, 1981-82 thru 1983-84, 168 games

Frederic Chabot: Montreal, Philadelphia, 1990-91 thru 1998-99, 32 games

Shawn Chambers: Minnesota, Washington, Tampa Bay, New Jersey, 1987-88 thru 1999-2000, 625 games

Alain Chevrier: New Jersey, Pittsburgh, Chicago, 1985-86 thru 1990-91, 234 games

Igor Chibirev: Hartford, 1993-94 thru 1994-95, 45 games

Phil Crowe: Los Angeles, Philadelphia, Nashville, 1993-94 thru 1999-2000, 94 games

Don Cutts: Edmonton, 1979-80, 6 games

Dave Duerden: Florida, 1999-2000, 2 games

Tom Draper: Winnipeg, Buffalo, New York Islanders, 1988-89 thru 1995-96, 53 games

Roy Edwards: Detroit, 1968-69 thru 1973-74, 236 games

John Emmons: Ottawa, Tampa Bay, Boston, 1999-2000 thru 2001-02, 85 games

Bob Essensa: Winnipeg, Detroit, Edmonton, Phoenix, Vancouver, Buffalo, 1988-89 thru 2001-02, 446 games

Chris Felix: Washington, 1987-88 thru 1990-91, 35 games

John Ferguson: Montreal, 1963-64 thru 1970-71, 500 games

Bob Fitchner: Quebec, 1979-80 thru 1980-81, 78 games (414 WHA games)

Mark Fitzpatrick: Los Angeles, New York Islanders, Florida, Tampa Bay, Chicago, Carolina, 1988-89 thru 1999-2000, 76 games (329 games overall)

Steve Fletcher: Montreal, Winnipeg, 1987-88 thru 1988-89, 3 games

Steve Gainey: Dallas, Phoenix, 2000-01 thru 2005-06, 33 games

Jamie Gallimore: Minnesota, 1977-78, 2 games

Sean Gauthier: San Jose, 1988-89, 1 game

Ken Gernander: New York Rangers, 1995-96 thru 2003-04, 12 games

Randy Gilhen: Hartford, Winnipeg, Pittsburgh, Los Angeles, New York Rangers, Tampa Bay, Florida, 1982-83 thru 1995-96, 457 games

Dirk Graham: Minnesota, Chicago, 1983-84 to 1994-95, 772 games

Trevor Halverson: Washington, 1998-99, 17 games

Justin Hodgman: Arizona, 2014-15, 5 games

Paul Hoganson: Pittsburgh, 1970-71, 2 games (142 WHA games)

Bill Houlder: Washington, Buffalo, Anaheim, St. Louis, Tampa Bay, San Jose, Nashville, 1987-88 thru 2002-03, 846 games

Jim Hrycuik: Washington, 1974-75, 21 games

Robbie Irons: St. Louis, 1968-69, 1 game

Steve Janaszak: Minnesota, Colorado, 1979-80 thru 1981-82, 3 games

Bob Janecyk: Chicago, Los Angeles, 1983-84 thru 1988-89, 110 games

Bobby Jay: Los Angeles, 1993-94, 3 games

Grant Jennings: Washington, Hartford, Pittsburgh, Toronto, 1987-88 thru 1995-96, 389 games

Duane Joyce: Dallas, 1993-94, 3 games

Kevin Kaminski: Washington, Minnesota, Quebec, 1988-89 thru 1996-97, 139 games

Ed Kastelic: Washington, Hartford, 1985-86 thru 1991-92, 220 games

Rick Knickle: Los Angeles, 1992-93 thru 1993-94, 14 games

Robbie Laird: Minnesota, 1979-80, 1 game

Dan Lambert: Quebec, 1990-91 through 1991-92, 29 games

Gord Lane: Washington, New York Islanders, 1975-76 thru 1984-85, 540 games

Jim Leavins: Detroit, New York Rangers, 1985-86 thru 1986-87, 41 games

Ray LeBlanc: Chicago, 1991-92, 1 game

Randy Legge: New York Rangers, 1972-73, 12 games

Lonnie Loach: Ottawa, Los Angeles, Anaheim, 1992-93 thru 1993-94, 56 games

Ken Lockett: Vancouver, 1974-75 thru 1975-76, 55 games (45 WHA games)

Dwayne Loudermilk: Washington, 1990-91, 2 games

Kevin MacDonald: Ottawa, 1992-93, 1 game

Jeff MacMillan: Dallas, 2003-04, 4 games

Bernie MacNeil: St. Louis, 1973-74, 4 games (119 WHA games)

Con Madigan: St. Louis, 1972-73, 20 games

Bruce Major: Quebec, 1990-91, 4 games

Steve Maltais: Washington, Minnesota, Tampa Bay, Detroit, Columbus, 1989-90 thru 2000-01, 120 games

Craig Martin: Winnipeg, Florida, 1994-95 thru 1996-97, 21 games

Spencer Martin: Colorado, 2016-17, 3 games

Darrell May: St. Louis, 1985-86 thru 1987-88, 6 games

Dunc McCallum: New York Islanders, Pittsburgh, 1965-66 thru 1970-71, 187 games (100 WHA games)

Mike McNeill: Chicago, Quebec, 1990-91 thru 1991-92, 63 games

Max Middendorf: Quebec, Edmonton, 1986-87 thru 1990-91, 3 games (13 overall)

Gerry Minor: Vancouver, 1979-80 thru 1983-84, 140 games

Glenn Mulvenna: Pittsburgh, Philadelphia, 1991-92 thru 1992-93, 2 games

Rob Murray: Washington, Winnipeg, Phoenix, 1989-90 thru 1998-99, 107 games

David Nemirovsky: Florida, 1995-96 thru 1998-99, 2 games (91 overall)

Igor Nikulin: Anaheim, 1996-97, 1 game

Bill Orban: Chicago, Minnesota, 1967-68 thru 1969-70, 114 games

Mike O'Neill: Winnipeg, Anaheim, 1991-92 thru 1996-97, 21 games

Dan Ratushny: Vancouver, 1992-93, 1 game

Alain Raymond: Washington, 1987-88, 1 game

Pokey Reddick: Winnipeg, Edmonton, Florida, 1986-87 thru 1993-94, 132 games

Todd Reirden: Edmonton, St. Louis, Atlanta, Phoenix, 1998-99 thru 2003-04, 183 games

Dave Richardson: New York Rangers, Chicago, Detroit, 1963-64 thru 1967-68, 45 games

Bobby Rivard: Pittsburgh, 1967-68, 27 games

Russ Romaniuk: Winnipeg, Philadelphia, 1995-96, 75 games (102 overall)

Len Ronson: New York Rangers, Oakland, 1960-61 thru 1968-69, 18 games

Andre Roy: Boston, Ottawa, Tampa Bay, Pittsburgh, Calgary, 1995-96 thru 2008-09, 502 games (515 overall)

Duane Rupp: New York Rangers, Toronto, Minnesota, Pittsburgh, 1962-63 thru 1972-73, 374 games (115 WHA games)

Ryan Savoia: Pittsburgh, 1998-99, 3 games

Dwight Schofield: Detroit, Montreal, St. Louis, Pittsburgh, Winnipeg, 1976-77 thru 1987-88, 209 games (211 overall)

Wally Schreiber: Minnesota, 1987-88 thru 1988-89, 41 games

Sean Selmser: Columbus, 2000-01, 1 game

Konstantin Shafranov: St. Louis, 1996-97, 5 games

Paul Shmyr: Chicago, Calgary, Minnesota, Hartford, 1968-69 thru 1981-82, 343 games (511 WHA games)

Bruce Shoebottom: Boston, 1987-88 thru 1990-91, 35 games

Peter Sidorkiewicz: Hartford, Ottawa, New Jersey, 1987-88 thru 1993-94, 246 games

Lee Sorochan: Calgary, 1998-99 thru 1999-2000, 3 games

Brian Stapleton: Washington, 1975-76, 1 game

Rick Tabaracci: Pittsburgh, Winnipeg, Washington, Calgary, Tampa Bay, Atlanta, Colorado, 1988-89 thru 1999-2000, 286 games

Greg Tebbutt: Quebec, Pittsburgh, 1979-80 thru 1983-84, 24 games (26 overall)

Floyd Thomson: St. Louis, 1971-72 thru 1979-80, 411 games

Brad Tiley: Phoenix, Philadelphia, 1997-98 thru 2000-01, 11 games

Nikolai Tsulygin: Anaheim, 1996-97, 22 games

Vladimir Tsyplakov: Los Angeles, Buffalo, 1995-96 thru 2000-01, 331 games

Rob Tudor: Vancouver, St. Louis, 1978-79 thru 1982-83, 28 games

Igor Ulanov: Winnipeg, Washington, Chicago, Tampa Bay, Montreal, Edmonton, New York Rangers, Florida, 1991-92 thru 2005-06, 656 games (739 overall)

Sid Veysey: Vancouver, 1977-78, 1 game

Lance Ward: Florida, Anaheim, 2000-01 thru 2003-04, 209

games

Kevin Weekes: Florida, Vancouver, New York Islanders, Tampa Bay, Carolina, New York Rangers, New Jersey, 1997-98 thru 2008-09, 348 games

Bob Wilkie: Detroit, Philadelphia, 1990-91 thru 1993-94, 10 games (18 overall)

Roman Will: Colorado, 2015-16, 1 game

Ron Zanussi: Minnesota, Toronto, 1977-78 thru 1981-82, 299 games

Most NHL games played by a former Komet

1. Bill Houlder 846
2. Dirk Graham 772
3. Igor Ulanov 656
4. Eric Boulton 654
5. Shawn Chambers 625
6. Gord Lane 540
7. Andre Roy 502
8. John Ferguson 500
9. Randy Gilhen 457
10. Bob Essensa 446
11. Floyd Thomson 411
12. Grant Jennings 389
13. Duane Rupp 374
14. Kevin Weekes 348
15. Paul Shmyr 343
16. Vladimir Tsyplakov 331
17. Ron Zanussi 299
18. Murray Bannerman 289
19. Rick Tabaracci 285

20. Peter Sidorkiewicz 246
21. Roy Edwards. 236
22. Alain Chevrier 234
23. Ed Kastelic 220
24. Dwight Schofield 209
25. Lance Ward 209
26. Les Binkley 192
27. Dunc McCallum 187
28. Todd Reirden 183
29. Tim Bergland 182
30. Eric Boguniecki 178

Most NHL games played before Komets

1. John Anderson 814
2. Andrew McBain 608
3. Doug Wickenheiser 556
4. Pat Elynuik 506
5. Al Sims 476
6. Tim Cheveldae 340
7. Paul Broten 322
8. Shawn Cronin. 292
9. Mark Fitzpatrick 263
10. Doug McCaig 263
11. Rik Wilson 251
12. Roman Oksiuta. 153
13. Brad Jones 148
14. Bob Mason 145
15. Bruce Boudreau 141
16. Rick St. Croix 130
17. Jean-Marc Lanthier. 105

CHAPTER 33

The best of the Komets to play in the NHL

Part of the Fort Wayne Komets' rich history comes from helping more than 110 players advance to the National Hockey League.

Here's a list of the former Komets who had the best careers in the NHL. To qualify, players had to play in Fort Wayne before they advanced to the NHL and had to be a Komet for at least 40 games, so NHL mainstays such as Dirk Graham, Shawn Chambers, Gord Lane, Eric Boulton, Kevin Weekes and Igor Ulanov don't count.

John Ferguson (Komets 1959-60): Obviously the MVP of a Komets-based NHL team with five Stanley Cups during an eight-year career with the Montreal Canadiens. He played 500 games, scoring 341 points and earning almost 1,500 penalty minutes as a right wing. He deserves to be inducted into the Hockey Hall of Fame someday.

Bob Fitchner (Komets 1971-73): After helping the Komets win the 1973 Turner Cup, the center played 414 games in the World Hockey Association and 78 in the NHL. He helped Quebec win the WHA title in 1977. He scored 239 major league points.

Bob Fitchner

Courtesy of The News-Sentinel

Bill Houlder (Komets 1987-88): The defenseman played 846 games in the NHL with Washington, Buffalo,

Anaheim, St. Louis, Tampa Bay, San Jose and Nashville. He scored 250 career points.

Dunc McCallum (Komets 1960-61): McCallum played 100 games in the WHA and 187 in the NHL as a defenseman with Pittsburgh and the New York Rangers.

Duane Rupp (Komets 1958-1960): The defenseman was one of the players who benefited greatly from the NHL's 1967 expansion, but he stayed in the NHL for 384 games and also played 122 games in the WHA. He might have played more, but he was buried in the Toronto Maple Leafs organization for several years.

Paul Shmyr (Komets 1966-67): As a defenseman, Shmyr was one of the more prolific scoring former Komets at the next level with more than 400 points in more than 800 games in the NHL and WHA.

Ron Zanussi (Komets 1976-77): Zanussi scored 53 goals with the Komets, and the winger continued to score at the next level, with 135 points in 299 games with Minnesota and Toronto.

Floyd Thomson (Komets 1969-70): The left wing played 421 games, all with the St. Louis Blues, mostly on a checking line.

Randy Gilhen (Komets 1985-86): The center already had played two games in the NHL with Hartford before coming to Fort Wayne, where he found his scoring touch. He then played 490 games in the NHL with Winnipeg, Pittsburgh, Los Angeles, Tampa Bay and the New York Rangers. He won a Stanley Cup with Pittsburgh in 1991.

Murray Bannerman (Komets 1977-78): The goaltender played in 328 NHL games with the Chicago Black Hawks and one with the Vancouver Canucks. He won 126 games and had a 3.83 goals-against average, which was pretty good during the high-scoring era in which he played.

Vladimir Tsyplakov
Courtesy of The News-Sentinel

Vladimir Tsyplakov (Komets 1993-95): Perhaps the best Komet to make it to the NHL from the last 25 years, the left wing played 331 games with Los Angeles and Buffalo, scoring 170 points.

Pokey Reddick (Komets 1985-86, 1991-93 and 1998-99): Reddick played only 136 games in the NHL, but he is the only Komet to win both a Turner Cup and a Stanley Cup. He was the backup goalie on Edmonton's 1990 championship team to cap a career that also saw him play with Winnipeg and Florida.

Bob Essensa (Komets 1988-89 and 1995-96): We're going with three goaltenders on our team because the position is so deep in the Komets' history, and Essensa deserves to be on the team. During a 12-year NHL career, he had a 3.15 goals-against average playing on teams that frankly weren't very good. He also rebuilt his career after getting destroyed in Detroit.

That group would make a pretty good team, but they probably wouldn't be able to touch a team of Komets who played previously in the NHL before coming to Fort Wayne. The forward lines on that team would have to include John Anderson, Bruce Boudreau, Andrew McBain, Doug Wickenheiser, Brad Jones, John LeBlanc and Pat Elynuik, while the defense would have to include Doug McCaig, Shawn Cronin, Al Sims and Hector Marini. We'd fudge on the rules a little bit with the goaltenders to have Mark Fitzpatrick and Tim Cheveldae.

It's always a fun topic to debate.

CHAPTER 34

Laird shared Stanley Cup with Fort Wayne

Rob Laird

Courtesy of The News-Sentinel

Though he'd secretly been working in the gym to make sure he could lift it, when Robbie Laird's turn came June 11, 2012, his adrenalin made the Stanley Cup seem weightless.

"I've watched this celebration for countless years, and to finally partake in it was a little unreal," the former Komets player and coach said. "You just want to hoist it and kiss it and pass it on. It's something I'll never forget."

Because he's the senior pro scout for Los Angeles, Laird was on the ice in 2012 as the Kings celebrated after ousting the New Jersey Devils in six games.

"The real emotions for me came about a week before with all the different feelings that you have, starting with feeling really good about the team and having a chance to win," Laird said. "I've had so many different calls and texts from people in the business. They all had a lot of good words. That's probably the neatest thing about this. I've reconnected with a lot of people that I haven't chatted with in quite a while."

It's only because of Laird's persistence that he still had a chance at the Cup. A 19-year-old seventh-round draft pick from Regina, Saskatchewan, by the Pittsburgh Penguins in 1974, Laird broke his wrist in three places during his first day of training camp. The Penguins sent him home to heal and then to Fort Wayne, where he became a legend because of his hustle and tenacity.

He played in only one National Hockey League game, getting called up in an emergency by the Minnesota North Stars. On Feb. 26, 1980, Laird skated 10 minutes against the Vancouver Canucks. He didn't get his picture taken or get to keep his jersey afterward, and he also never got another chance.

Five years later, Laird started his coaching career with the Komets. He worked his way through the minors again to become an assistant coach with the Washington Capitals and started in the Kings' system in 1994. No one in the hockey office has been with the Kings longer than Laird.

As a scout, he helped the Kings sign many of the players on their 2012 and 2014 championship teams. His goal was always to help a team win the Stanley Cup.

The week before the Kings won their first title in 2012, Laird started writing down everyone he had worked with in the Kings' organization over the previous 18 years. Then he thought about all the people from Fort Wayne who'd had an influence on his life.

"Once you are in the hockey business, it's the ultimate goal from the time you are a kid," Laird said. "It's satisfying. I really felt fortunate to be in this position. You have to be lucky, and the timing has to be right. I was really so fortunate, more than anything."

As a scout, Laird looks for skills, character, hockey sense, speed and toughness. He'll talk with a player's coaches, local media, anyone who can give him a read on a player.

"I look at each player on each team, as difficult as that is,'" Laird said. "Some players, you have a history of and you don't have to focus on them as much."

After 18 years, he had the most seniority of any member of the Kings' hockey department – while also finding time to watch a few Komets games each season. He's one of three Kings scouts who focus on the pro side, covering the National Hockey League, American Hockey League and ECHL along with occasional trips to Europe.

His main job is to find talent the Kings might acquire through free agency, waiver claims or trades. He'll usually focus on 12 players per game and can watch three or four players each shift. He concentrates on 10 NHL teams and will watch them for as many as six to 10 games during a season.

By the end of a season, he'll have at least two reports on every player in the league. The three pro scouts constantly collaborate on the reports.

"Sometimes you get sent on a specific mission, like maybe we're talking to this team and this player may be available," he said. "When he's on the ice, I don't take my eyes off him. In the early part of the year, we're trying to build a list of the top players at all their positions and then break it down by player type. Then the closer you get to the trading deadline, you're looking at specific players, and then after that, you want to focus in more on free agent players."

Laird estimates he flies more than 100,000 miles and drives more than 25,000 miles during a season, spending more than 100 nights in hotels. Winning two Stanley Cup rings made his entire career worthwhile.

During their 2012 run, the Kings led each of their first three series 3-0 and needed only 14 games to reach the Stanley Cup Finals against New Jersey. They also built a 3-0 lead against the Devils before winning the title in Game 6.

The run to the 2014 title was much different. The Kings trailed San Jose 3-0 before rallying to win the next four games. Then they trailed Anaheim 3-2, losing three straight games, before again rallying to win in seven games. Finally, they had to win a Game 7 in Chicago after almost blowing a 3-1 series lead in the Western Conference finals before beating the New York Rangers in five games in the Stanley Cup Finals. The Kings' 26-game playoff run was the longest in NHL history.

"I'm every bit as excited," Laird said at the time. "These games have been a roller coaster. It's a totally different feeling than last time when I didn't start to feel the nerves until the finals."

CHAPTER 35

Former Komets had opinions on NHL's best player ever

Mario Lemieux and Wayne Gretzky are simply the greatest hockey players ever, but which was better?

Who better to ask than a panel of goaltenders? Their answers were interesting.

"It's like comparing two great paintings and asking which is the most beautiful," said former Komet Stephane Beauregard. "You have to appreciate both players for what they accomplished and how they dominated. I kind of find it kind of sad to pick."

Beauregard played several games a year against Lemieux as a member of the Philadelphia Flyers and several as a Winnipeg Jet against Gretzky. The first time he played Gretzky, Beauregard said he couldn't take his eyes off The Great One during warm-ups.

"Mario might be the best one-on-one player, but Gretzky was the mastermind behind those great Edmonton teams," Beauregard said. "The most extraordinary thing is they have rough nights like everyone else, but they still end up with two points."

Tom Draper has probably had the most success against Gretzky. Gretzky never scored against Draper, but Lemieux has lit him up like a flashlight.

"The first game I ever played in the NHL was with Winnipeg, and Lemieux had three breakaways on me and scored on the third one," Draper said. "I really think individually Lemieux is a better player because he's bigger, stronger and a much better skater than most players. He also has a better shot than Gretz."

How did Draper prepare for a game against Lemieux or Gretzky?

"In my case, I always tried not to pay attention to who has the puck, but you're always aware of them," Draper said. "There's not a whole lot you can do."

The one player in the survey who picked Gretzky was ex-Komet Pokey Reddick, who played against Gretzky as a member of the Winnipeg Jets and Edmonton Oilers.

"Gretzky could totally control and dominate a game all by himself," Reddick said. "When he came in, no one had any idea or strategy for stopping him. He could win games against good teams all by himself. Some people are blessed with talent, and he certainly is one of those people."

Gretzky holds the NHL records for career goals, assists and points, but Lemieux actually averaged more goals per game. Lemieux also missed more than 500 games because of injuries and illness. He missed four seasons to fight Hodgkin's' lymphoma. He also didn't have Gretzky's incredible Edmonton roster of talent to play with. The Oilers were so good they won the Stanley Cup the year after Gretzky left, with Reddick serving as their back-up.

Pokey Reddick
Courtesy of The News-Sentinel

Maybe the biggest argument is that while Lemieux changed the game, Gretzky changed the world of hockey like no one before or since.

Several former Komets had up-close experiences with Gretzky.

Goaltender Bruce Racine was playing in St. Louis during the 1995-96 season when Gretzky arrived from Los Angeles via a trade with 18 games left in the regular season.

"I remember the first time he came in, I was in the dressing room stretching," Racine said. "He was in his stall taping his stick, and I was watching him in awe. He looked up and saw me looking at him, so I looked away. Then he went back to taping his stick, and I looked up staring at him, and he looked at me again. I was like, 'I have to move.'"

That's the reaction most of the Komets have when talking of their brushes with The Great One. Mike Martin played with Gretzky in the New York Rangers' 1997 training camp. A natural defenseman, Martin was moved to forward and his boyhood idol was his center.

"I was pretty nervous, especially playing up on forward with the greatest center ever to play the game," Martin said. "When I saw my name next to his (on the lineup board), it was just unbelievable. It didn't look right, but I got over that and it was a lot of fun. He's a nice guy, and he made me feel comfortable and he helped me out by talking to me in the dressing room."

Former Komet Adam Smith said Gretzky had the ability to take over a locker room without saying anything because everyone knew where he was at all times.

"He's got so much presence," Smith said. "So many things are different when he's around. There's an aura about the whole camp and about the whole dressing room. He's not the most vocal guy, but when he decides it's time to stand up and say something, you can hear a pin drop. He just demands that much respect."

Reddick played against Gretzky in Winnipeg and was traded to Edmonton in 1988, the year after Gretzky was traded to Los Angeles. As good as he was on the ice, Reddick also noticed that Gretzky is just as great off the ice.

"I remember he always walked around with two dozen sticks after the games, and I asked the trainer what he was doing with an armful of sticks," Reddick said. "He always gives them to kids who are hanging around. You can't say anything against him. All you can do is be thankful you either got to play against him or if you played with him. The guy is unreal."

Reddick's son Bryce has a stick autographed from Gretzky, as does Racine, but Martin and Smith said they felt uneasy about asking for one. Each Gretzky stick is numbered, and Racine's is the 37th stick used in St. Louis. Racine has a better memory than any souvenir.

"Later on in the playoffs that year, just by chance, he and I showed up at the same hotel restaurant at the same time and we got to have lunch together," Racine said. "I'm sure he doesn't even remember, but I'll never forget it, and he ended up buying.

"Watching his last game (in 1999), it was pretty special just knowing I had gotten to hang out with him for just a couple of days. I still shake my head. That's a memory I'll never forget."

CHAPTER 36

Lester Patrick Award stunned Chase to silence

Bob Chase with Lester Patrick Award
Courtesy of Tara Pembroke

It took cooperation from the National Hockey League and USA Hockey to keep Bob Chase quiet for two weeks.

On Aug. 28, 2012, while driving his pickup and towing a massive fifth-wheel RV, the Komets broadcaster was dodging the traffic flying by on I-65 in Tennessee. Chase and his wife, Murph, were riding home from visiting family in Huntsville, Ala., when the cell phone rang at 10 a.m. "Bob, it's somebody for you," Murph said, handing him the phone.

"Is this Bob Chase?" the voice on the other end said. "Thank goodness I finally found you. I've been trying for over a week to get in touch with you. This is Gary Bettman."

Instantly, Chase, then 86, started wondering why the NHL commissioner would want to talk to him.

"I wanted to be the first to let you know and congratulate you," Bettman said. "You have been chosen to receive the Lester Patrick Award for 2012."

Starting in 1966, the Lester Patrick Award has been presented by the NHL and USA Hockey as a lifetime achievement award for service to the sport in the United States. Past winners include Wayne Gretzky, Gordie Howe, Bobby Orr, Phil Esposito, former NHL commissioners and Olympic gold medal-winning teams – basically a Who's Who of the Hockey Hall of Fame. This would be comparable to an actor receiving a lifetime achievement award at the Oscars.

"While we're talking, everybody is going 70 miles per hour and I'm trying to keep the truck on the road with tears streaming down my face," Chase said. "I just kept driving because there was no way to get off the road."

One thing most of the winners have in common is they have been interviewed by Chase – whose real name is Wallenstein – during his then-59 seasons calling Komets games. Chase's run is the longest with any professional hockey team, breaking Foster Hewitt's run with the Toronto Maple Leafs from 1927 to 1963.

Perhaps no one ever introduced more people to hockey and maybe no one caused more people to love it than Chase.

Before 1995, WOWO's 50,000-watt radio signal could reach as far as the Canadian Maritimes, the U.S. East and Southeast coasts, and pretty far into the western sections of the country. About the only area WOWO didn't reach was a stretch between Portland, Ore., and Orange County, Calif., back to Fort Wayne because of the signal's direction and competition with other high-powered stations.

Players have said a perk of signing with Fort Wayne was that their parents could listen to all the games in their own living rooms.

Throughout the 1950s and much of the 1960s, WOWO and Chase were the only broadcast throughout the International Hockey League and the only hockey broadcast throughout much of the rest of the country. During an era where there were only six NHL teams, the game he saw was the only one to visualize for many young fans who would fall asleep listening to their transistor radio hidden under the covers.

Today, there are millions of hockey fans because Bob Chase introduced their parents, grandparents and maybe even great-grandparents to the game. That's why he won the award.

"The world would not ignore Bob Chase," said protégé Mike Emrick who grew up in LaFontaine listening to Chase. "(The award is) something that needed to happen, and I'm glad it's happening at a time when he can enjoy it. The important thing is the committee saw the gravity of this and decided it was important to get this done. I'm thrilled for him, and it could have come from 50 different directions. This was a campaign of many people."

Chase was presented the award Oct. 15, 2012, in Dallas at the U.S. Hockey Hall of Fame Induction Ceremony and Dinner, sharing the honor with Washington Capitals president Dick Patrick, grandson of Lester Patrick.

During the dinner, Chase and Patrick were interviewed by ESPN's Steve Levy, and Chase got to meet Hall of Fame

inductees Lou Lamoriello, Mike Modano and Eddie Olczyk.
"It had to be one of the most memorable moments in my life," Chase said. "You don't move to those heights very often when you spend your life in a sport like this. I'm glad I'll have pictures to help me remember it all. This was top-of-the-mountain stuff."

Along with his wife, Chase was joined by his daughter, Karin, and her husband, Vic; his son, David; former Komet Terry Pembroke and his daughter Tara; protégé and NBC broadcaster Mike Emrick; Komets owner Stephen Franke; and team president Michael Franke.

"It was a class act," Pembroke said. "They treated Chase royally, and probably 40 percent of the crowd was all professional NHL people. The number of people who came by and said they listened to Bob Chase when they were growing up was almost overwhelming."

Chase said he was a little surprised by the number of people who came up to talk, thank him and get their picture taken with him.

"It was just the most enjoyable night," he said. "The pomp and ceremony was pretty unrivaled. Having my name on the lips of a lot of pretty important people made me feel good. That was a once-in-a-lifetime night, and I'm glad it happened to me."

CHAPTER 37
McNeil's dream was a masterpiece

Bobby McNeil
Courtesy of Fort Wayne Komets

When cancer survivor Terry Fox started his heroic trek across Canada in 1980, he was hoping to inspire people. It certainly worked for former Komet Bob McNeil.

During Fox's iconic walk, he stopped in Toronto to have his picture taken with Maple Leafs captain Darryl Sittler. In 2011, a poster of that picture was awarded to McNeil, who scored nine goals and 22 points for the 1954-55 Komets, and who annually rollerbladed in the charity Terry Fox Run in Stouffville, Ontario.

McNeil came up with a plan to turn the poster into a major donation to fight cancer, persuading more than 150 current and former National Hockey League players to sign it. Former Chicago Blackhawk Peter Conacher suggested the idea to McNeil, who annually attended the NHL Legends Luncheon.

"There are signatures everywhere but on the heads," McNeil said in 2011. "It's getting full, but I can squeeze a few more on there."

Within the first 13 months, he had gotten autographs from Gordie Howe, Bobby Orr, Mario Lemieux, Don Cherry, Paul Coffey, Glenn Anderson, Bryan Trottier and even Sittler.

Bobby McNeil's wife Sheila and daughter Cindy show off his poster *Courtesy of McNeil family*

The other part of the story is that McNeil also was a cancer survivor. In 2009, while he was in the hospital with pneumonia, he asked one of the nurses what the lump on the back of his neck was. It was malignant melanoma.

A week after being released, he was playing over-70 hockey again. He usually put on the rollerblades for an hour to 90 minutes each day.

Unfortunately, McNeil became sick with another form of cancer, brain cancer, which cost him his life in 2013 at age 79. He left the poster to his wife, Sheila, and daughter, Cindy.

Because McNeil would never let the poster out of his presence, he refused to fly with it, and the only signature he'd been unable to get was Mark Messier. There was some talk about maybe stopping the project, but McNeil's oncologist encouraged Cindy to keep going until he could get Messier's signature.

That meant getting some help and simply waiting until the right opportunity for Messier to come closer to the poster. Then Canadian TV broadcaster and family friend Lance Brown told Cindy that Messier would be appearing in Toronto. Brown filled Messier in on the poster's backstory and asked whether he'd be willing to sign it.

"We were already on our way down there, and I had decided not to take no for an answer," Cindy said. "Mark sat with me and my niece and nephew and was just a very classy guy. I was very emotional."

More than a year after his death, the first part of McNeil's mission was completed. Cindy even persuaded Fox's father, Rolly, to add his signature. The finished product contained 177 signatures, including 33 Hall of Fame members and all of McNeil's doctors. Another surprise came when Sittler arranged to see the finished poster. McNeil himself said in 2011 that the poster would be priceless because it is one-of-a-kind.

"Cindy did not give up on this," Sheila said. "She's like her dad. Bob would be absolutely over the moon about this."

With advice from McNeil's friend Richard Kelly, Sheila and Cindy took the poster to a Toronto framer who treated it with spectacular care. Then they held an open house for friends and family to see the completed work.

"The real thing is pretty remarkable," Cindy said. "Somebody suggested we keep it as a memento, but that is not what my dad wanted. It's just very overwhelming. Now that we even have it in the frame, it's not complete. When we get a check for the Terry Fox Foundation, then (it will) feel complete."

The story finally had a happy ending. An anonymous donor offered $20,000, and the poster was installed at McNeil's hometown rink, the Stouffville Arena in Ontario. A small copy of the poster is also hanging in the hospital where McNeil was treated to inspire others battling cancer and as a testament to his doctors.

"It looks like my dad's pride and joy project is coming to an end," Cindy McNeil said. "I am sure he is smiling from above!"

CHAPTER 38

Maintaining Tampa Bay's ice takes a Miracle

Tom Miracle

Courtesy of Tampa Bay Lightning

When NHL commentators Jeremy Roenick and Barry Melrose made some critical observations during the 2015 NHL playoffs about the Tampa Bay ice conditions, a Fort Wayne native got very upset. Tom Miracle worked at least 12 hours a day during the playoffs to make sure the Tampa Bay Lightning's ice was perfect, which isn't easy considering he could hit a golf ball from the arena and smack a nearby cruise ship in the Gulf of Mexico.

"We have our challenges here," said Miracle, a North Side High School graduate, "but I have a staff of 15 that works very hard to make sure this ice is as good as any in the league. We work very hard at it."

Miracle started as a 14-year-old stick boy with the Komets working with coaches such as Gregg Pilling and Moose Lallo, and later he went to work for Memorial Coliseum Vice President of Operations Bryan Christie.

After moving to Tampa, Fla., in 1994, he was working at Busch Gardens when he noticed someone wearing a Las Vegas Thunder hat. Tim Friedenberger turned out to be the lead ice technician for the new Tampa Bay arena and hired Miracle on

Sept. 6, 1996, for $7.50 an hour. The Lightning started their first training camp that month.

Miracle has worked 25 years with the Lightning, now as the ice operations manager, and has a Stanley Cup ring from the team's 2004 championship.

Making the ice is the easy part, even when the outside temperature is 93 degrees. Maintaining the quality requires the real work. Twelve hours before opening faceoff, the building starts a cool-down to 58 degrees and 42 percent humidity in an attempt to counter the body heat of 19,500 fans.

"The building is a positive-pressure area, which means it pushes out rather than allowing all that heat to come in, but the human body brings in heat and humidity," Miracle said. "The first period is trying to let the building recover, and second and third periods are when we really do our best."

Miracle checks his computer system three times per period and makes adjustments throughout the game based on building temperature, the concrete under the ice and the ice quality. The crew also shovels the entire surface in two minutes during every timeout.

"I work real close with the officials, and every time they come off the ice, someone will tell me how it's going," he said. "It's a science, and you have to play the numbers and the conditions and how hard they are playing the game. If it's a one-goal game, those guys are playing hard. There are so many different variables."

Being in control of the ice means sometimes Miracle has to make some people mad, demanding that they open doors to the outside as little as possible. Game days usually last 14 hours, so many that the building general manager asked whether he needed to reserve a hotel room for Miracle.

"Friends ask me all the time if I'm excited for the finals," Miracle said. "I tell them that I do the same thing for a preseason game as I do for a Stanley Cup Final, the best I can do. It's just another game to me, and I handle it as such. I do what I have to do, whether it's a preseason game or Game 7, and that's all I can do."

CHAPTER 39

Wissman's NHL career lasted behind the scenes

A few years ago, a former NHL player was assigned to the Komets, and one day he decided to show the team equipment manager how things are supposed to be done in his locker.

"This is how things are done in the show," the player instructed.

The equipment manager just nodded his head respectfully, kept his mouth shut and walked away.

One of the Komets who had been around longer than five minutes, leaned over and smacked the offending player on the back of the head. "Dude, that guy's got 10 times more games in the NHL than you do!"

"That guy" was Steve "Swiss" Wissman, who has probably seen more National Hockey League games than anyone in Fort Wayne history, and he had one of the best possible seats.

From 2002 to 2009, Wissman worked the St. Louis Blues bench as the team's assistant equipment manager. He worked everything from exhibitions to playoff games, finishing with more than 400 games before a freak injury forced him to retire.

Wissman started out as a goalie with the old Junior Pepsi Komets and on the Harding High School club team. He was a stick boy under coach Ron Ullyot in the early 1980s, and then coach Rob Laird hired him for his first real job as the Komets'

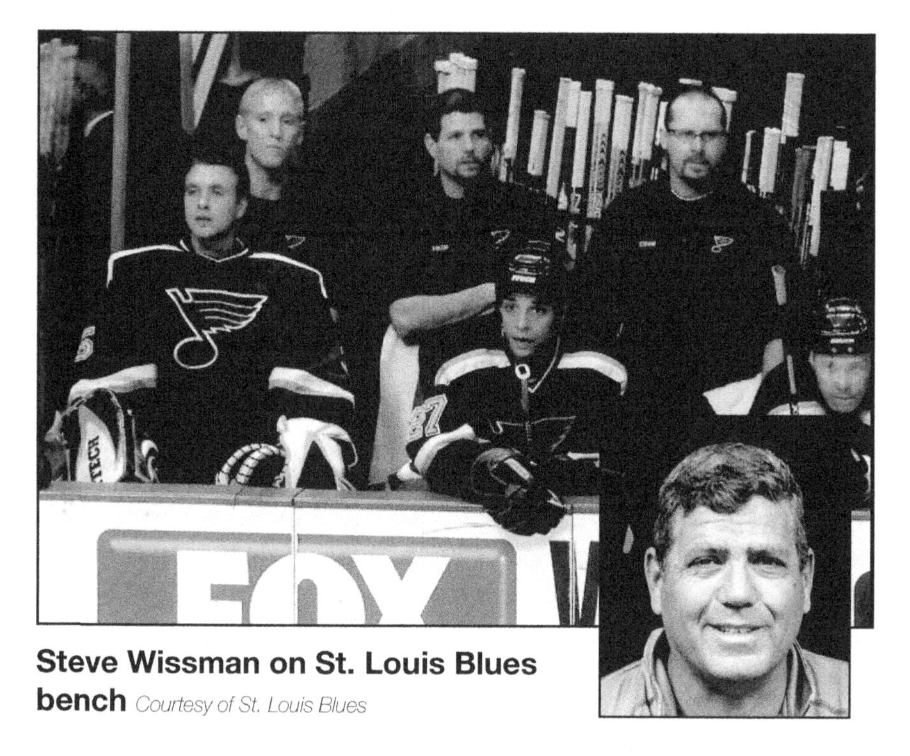

Steve Wissman on St. Louis Blues bench *Courtesy of St. Louis Blues*

trainer/equipment manager in the late 1980s. Eventually, Wissman worked for 13 teams, including six seasons in the National Hockey League with the Blues.

Along the way, his career led him to Phoenix for two years; to Tri-Cities, Wash., for two; to Las Vegas for one; back to Phoenix for three; to Kalamazoo for three; and to Kansas City for one more before he took a year off to work for a deck company in Fort Wayne. He then went back into hockey in Cleveland for a year before joining the Blues.

"I spent my whole life wanting to work for the Komets, listening to Bob Chase in the comforts of my bedroom, and my favorite NHL team was actually the St. Louis Blues," Wissman said. "I was a kid with large dreams that I thought would never come true. ... When people ask me where I am from, I am proud to say, 'Fort Wayne, Indiana, home of the Komets!'"

Wissman also was involved in one of the oddest "future considerations" deals in Komets history. Before the 1996-97 season, forward Andy Bezeau was upset with the Komets and demanded a trade, even going so far as to attend training camp with the Michigan K-Wings. The K-Wings and Komets were trying to work out a trade when things got very strange.

When the Phoenix Roadrunners folded the year before, the K-Wings hired Wissman as their equipment manager, and he brought several truckloads of supplies with him, including the Roadrunners' washers and dryers. He knew the Komets' washers and dryers were almost worn out, so he called Fort Wayne equipment manager Joe Franke to ask if he wanted the dryers.

Franke told the Komets front office about the possibility, and talks started with the K-Wings. Eventually, the Komets traded Bezeau's rights to Kalamazoo for "future considerations," which turned out to be two dryers worth about $1,600 apiece.

After Bezeau had played one game in Michigan, the IHL voided the trade – though no one can remember why – so the Komets ended up buying the dryers.

Eventually, he worked his way up to St. Louis, and part of Wissman's duties included packing the equipment in the locker room, loading it onto the truck after games, then making sure everything got to the airport and onto the team's chartered plane. He was walking around the truck at Los Angeles International early during the 2006-07 season when a bag of sticks fell over and landed on his head.

It took him 14 months to recover enough to resume all his duties. He came back, but an errant puck during warm-ups nailed him above the left eyebrow. He woke up in a Columbus, Ohio, hospital but couldn't tell the doctors where he was simply because the NHL schedule is such a blur.

At that point in his career, Wissman had worked 1,801 professional games (not including another 500 junior games).

"It was fun, though," he said. "I remember my first (NHL) game, holy cow, there (were) 20,000 people, and I was a little jittery. I remember I thought the guys were just flying. After you get into a routine, the game is just like you are used to. What was nice was waking up in the morning and looking forward to going to work."

In 2010, he suffered a heart attack and underwent a triple bypass surgery.

"It was actually a blessing in disguise that I got my concussions, because if I wouldn't have, I probably would have died in a hotel or at the rink," he said. "In this job, you are always tired, so you don't know the effects."

An equipment manager's hours are brutal. When he was in St. Louis, Wissman often arrived at 7 a.m. and didn't leave until midnight – unless the Blues were traveling the next day, and then he'd just sleep at the rink.

To help with his recovery and to get closer to family, Wissman and his wife, Barbara, and their sons Adam and Corey moved back to Fort Wayne. After Wissman healed, he started to get the hockey itch again and reached out to Joe Franke to see if he needed any help around the rink.

The first time Wissman met Franke, Wissman was a 17-year-old junior goaltender for the Harding High School club hockey team who was asking the Komets' 22-year-old trainer/equipment manager for a job. It would take almost 30 years before they actually worked together.

After starting as a 17-year-old stick boy, Franke began working full time for the Komets in 1979, fresh out of Bishop Dwenger High School. In 1985, former Komets coach Ron Ullyot asked him to come to Indianapolis to work in the Central Hockey League. A few months later, Wissman became Franke's replacement with the Komets and coach Robbie Laird.

As of the summer of 2017, Franke has worked more than 3,000 pro games, and he helped Wissman reach the 2,000-game mark in 2013. It's kind of a cool job because Wissman does all the stuff behind the scenes that nobody knows about but that has to be done for a hockey team to function. Part of that includes dealing with player superstitions and being ready for anything new that pops up.

He said the key to surviving and enjoying the job is to laugh every day. Good seasons fly by, bad seasons drag worse than poor marriages.

The job gets a little tougher when a team is struggling.

"When the team is winning, everything is great," Wissman said. "When the team is losing, they are looking for all the answers, especially the goalies. They are always looking to change something up to make it better."

It's Wissman's job to help them try something new, and hockey players are usually tremendously superstitious. When he was with the Blues, Wissman had a list of everything a player liked in his stall, from which side a towel should be hung to where drinks should be placed. Some players like having their stuff packed away by the staff, and some freak out if anyone looks at it.

"I wouldn't trade it, even if somebody said you could be a doctor and make a ton of money," Wissman said. "This isn't a real job. You don't have to punch a clock. I've had a lot of fun."

Wissman finally retired for good at the end of the 2013-14 season and now lives in Florida.

CHAPTER 40

Faber won three rings with the Blackhawks

When he was a kid growing up in Auburn, Ind., Brandon Faber and his buddies loved going to sporting events in Fort Wayne. Komets hockey, Fort Wayne Flames/Indiana Kick indoor soccer, Wizards baseball, Rhinos football and Fury basketball were the favorites.

"I'd watch any game at any time, no matter what sport it was or what time of year it was," Faber said. "Those were the coolest, pinch-me moments."

Oh, he's topped those quite a few times since.

Faber went to work for the Chicago Bulls in their communications department in 2002 before joining the Chicago Blackhawks as senior director of communications and community relations in 2008, the year after Jonathan Toews and Patrick Kane were drafted. It was pretty good timing considering the Blackhawks would win the Stanley Cup in 2010, 2013 and again in 2015.

"The coolest thing every time we've won is the parade through Chicago," Faber said. "I've been fortunate enough to be on the bus with the cup all three times. The first two years, my parents couldn't make it up, and in 2015 I said, 'Mom, Dad, do whatever you have to do to be here. This is the coolest thing you'll ever imagine.' After the parade, they still couldn't believe what just happened."

That's kind of been the life theme for Faber, who played football

Brandon Faber and family with Stanley Cup
Courtesy of Chicago Blackhawks

at DeKalb High School and was part of the Barons' 1994 state runner-up squad before graduating in 1997. He'd also regularly come to Fort Wayne with his buddies to work Fort Wayne Fury games for DeKalb graduate Scott Sproat, currently the Komets' executive vice president and co-owner.

"Scott allowed me to really kick-start things, just being a high school punk going down there and working those games and helping out with halftime or time-out promotions, running tickets around town or any of the stuff that he let us do," Faber said. "If he didn't do that, maybe I'm not where I am today."

Faber went to Indiana University to study secondary education with hopes of becoming a high school athletics director, but after his sophomore year, he changed his major to communications. After graduating in 2002, he took an internship with USA Basketball before hearing about an opening with the Bulls.

In 2008, he moved to the Blackhawks, and over nine seasons, he got to experience some wonderful things and work an amazing amount of hours.

"A lot of times, you don't even know it's a job," he said. "The things you get to see and do and be a part of are pretty special. I still talk to a lot of those guys on the Hawks pretty regularly. They are just good friends now. You spend that much time with people, especially with the success the team had ... those are high points for everybody's careers. You just have a special bond."

Faber also met his wife Melissa, a nurse practitioner from New Orleans who he married in 2011. In 2017, they have 5-year-old twins Riley and Jack with another baby on the way.

"Being from New Orleans, she never really knew anything about hockey," Faber said. "The first time she ever went ice skating was at Wrigley Field when we held the Winter Classic (in 2015). She didn't have the pleasure of going ice skating at Glenbrook Mall as a kid."

In 2016, Faber got the chance to return to his first love when the Chicago Bears reached out to him about becoming their vice president of communications. Having only 16 game days also gives him a little more consistent time at home and allows him to excel at what he's best at, working with people and solving problems.

"It's about timing, networking and creating relationships, and helping people and trying to return the favor whenever you can," he said. "It has a lot to do with my upbringing, the way my parents raised me and treating everyone with respect, and always helping anybody who asks you or needs your help, and never stop learning. That's the approach I've tried to take."

But what's next?

"I'm not even 40 yet, I've been in Chicago for 15 years and I've won three Stanley Cups. I've worked with the Bulls, the Blackhawks and now the Bears, and if you had told me 20 years ago when I was in DeKalb High School that I was going to have the chance to work at one of those, I wouldn't have believed you. I've couldn't be more blessed personally and professionally."

CHAPTER 41

Hodgman took atypical route to NHL

So what's it like to actually play in the National Hockey League? There's really only one Komet to ask.

When Justin Hodgman left the Komets after helping Fort Wayne win the International Hockey League's Turner Cup in 2010, he was determined to make it to the NHL. There was a second year remaining on an American Hockey League contract with the Toronto Marlies, and he thought he'd have a good chance.

But he led the Marlies in scoring yet never got a call-up. Then he broke his leg, and no one offered him another deal the next summer. His NHL dream was over.

"I gave up on it, to be honest with you," he said. "I said, 'All right, I'm not going to make it because I couldn't get a deal. Maybe it's because I didn't get drafted, but whatever it is, I'm not going to get a deal.' I had been at training camps and there was a little bit of interest, but never enough to get someone to pull the trigger on a deal. 'OK,' I said, 'I'm just going to go over to Europe.'"

He signed in Finland where he put together an outstanding season, scoring 53 points in 59 games. That earned him a two-year contract in Russia where he played for former NHL coaches Paul Maurice and then Mike Keenan. The deal gave him a little financial security and the confidence to try one more chance to make the NHL.

After receiving a training camp invite to the Arizona Coyotes,

Justin Hodgman
Courtesy of Arizona Coyotes

Hodgman worked into the best shape of his life, selling himself as a depth and a role player, someone who would do anything to help the team. In reality, as an undrafted 26-year-old few people had heard of, he was expected to be training camp fodder and moved along quickly.

But he kept surprising everyone.

"I went in early to show how I was ready, and I gave it my all," Hodgman said. "I just kept scoring, even in scrimmages. I just refused to let them send me down because I kept scoring. You want to stick around as long as you can, and if you keep scoring, they are not going to send you down."

After scoring once in the team's red vs. white scrimmage, Hodgman scored four goals and five points in five exhibition games. Teammate Keith Yandle joked, "Save them for October!"

Though he led the team in scoring during the preseason, Hodgman made the opening-day roster but was a healthy scratch for the first two regular-season games. The Coyotes had more proven players, and there were 14 forwards on the roster when only 12 play during a game.

With no room in the lineup, Hodgman was sent down to Portland of the American Hockey League. During the first three games, he was scoreless and was minus-3. He was only there for a few days when Arizona's David Moss broke his hand, and Portland coach Ray Edwards called Hodgman on Oct. 23 to tell him he was going back up.

"I said, 'Holy Crap, I don't know what to say, I can't believe it!'" Hodgman said.

The first thing he did? Pack a Halloween costume. He was figuring the Coyotes' team Halloween party would likely be held after the Oct. 25 home game against Florida, so he quickly put together a costume that allowed him to imitate the singer Pharrell.

"David Moss called me, actually," Hodgman said. "It was a class act by him because I was the guy replacing him. He said he had a Super Mario costume for me, but I said I already had something."

"Veteran move!" Moss said. "You got called up and you packed your suit, whatever (else) and a Halloween costume. Rare. Good veteran move."

But first, there was the game, Hodgman's first in the NHL.

Because of the way his training camp had gone, Hodgman was still confident, and coach Dave Tippett put him at center on the second line between Sam Gagner and Martin Erat.

"I remember the national anthem was pretty special on the bench," he said. "Just after, Dave Tippett came over and tapped me on the shoulder and said, 'Good luck, kid.' That was a special moment for sure."

He doesn't remember anything about his first shift but recalls making a good defensive move later during the period, moving down low to keep himself between the opposing center and the puck. He also won his first faceoff. He was buzzing, flying up and down the ice in a scoreless game.

"I was just playing a good, hard, simple game," he said. "I had maybe one shot on net and created one scoring chance, had a couple of hits. I took a penalty late in the first period which shouldn't have been. It was a tap on the hands. I've had it done to me a million times and never gotten a call. My heart rate went way up. My first thought was, 'At least I made the gamesheet,' and then it was, 'God, just please don't score.'"

The Panthers didn't, thanks to a Florida player quickly taking a hooking call, and the game remained scoreless through two periods.

"The adrenaline is going nuts," Hodgman recalled. "I remember feeling tired even though I was in shape and prepared. I think it was from over-adrenaline, which I let get to me too often when I was up there, unfortunately. I think I let that raw, 'Oh, my God, I'm here,' last too long, and that's what hurt me the most."

But not during the third period. Hodgman drew a tripping penalty against Florida's Sean Bergenheim 8:36 into the period to set up Arizona's sixth power play of the game.

He was feeling good watching his teammates on the power play when Tippett said he wanted Hodgman to go out at center with the second unit. He won the faceoff and made a good move to help bring the puck into the offensive zone.

"I couldn't believe this was happening. I felt like I belonged, but I was nervous as hell. It was almost a perfect storm. I drew the penalty, it was my first game, I was hot, I was the story of training camp, and I made a nice play at the blue line and I went to my spot. I'm trying to tell Keith Yandle to pass it over to Oliver Ekman-Larsson, but he shot it instead. Thank God he didn't listen."

Hodgman was setting up off the far post behind Florida goaltender Roberto Luongo when Yandle shot from the point. Luongo made the save, but Arizona's Lauri Korpikoski got the rebound in front.

"Most guys would have just tried to bang it, but he saw I was backdoor sniffing it out and he just tapped it to me," Hodgman said. "I had a four-by-six net to shoot at. It was just unbelievable. I couldn't believe it."

Hodgman couldn't miss, and he didn't before racing to the boards to leap against the glass. He got a massive high five from Yandle and kept smiling from ear to ear.
The goal tied the game 1-1, and the Coyotes eventually won in overtime as Ekman-Larsson scored a power-play goal.

Afterwards, the team gave Hodgman the championship belt as the game's hardest-working player, and Tippett gave him the coach's lineup card and the yellow copy of the official gamesheet.

The Halloween party helped Hodgman to settle down enough to sleep that night.

The next game was three days later at Tampa Bay, but until then, Hodgman got to experience real NHL life. It was a lot different from anywhere in the minors, and not just because the team traveled by private jet and not on a bus. Part of that includes the flight attendants providing a wine or a beer at each player's seat, along with an excellent meal.

"It's all just a step up," Hodgman said. "You show up in the morning and there's a chef there, and you put in your order and he'll make you whatever you want. This is in the room right across from the practice rink, and you show up and there's a spread, and there's a chef making eggs, too.

"The venues are state of the art. Practices are never really that hard because there are so many games. You are just trying to fine-tune things, and if you are not in shape, it will show and they send you down, so you don't need to bag skate. The passes are crisp and the expectations are high."

Though Hodgman's father and grandparents went to the game in Tampa, he didn't play. Tippett was likely trying to protect him against the high-flying Lightning who still scored seven goals in the game. After a first-period workout and some stat work during the second, Hodgman sat with his family during the third period.

That was kind of the start of the end of Hodgman's ride. He played two nights later at Florida but was robbed by Luongo.

"I played OK, but I didn't play great," Hodgman said. "It might have been a reality check for the team that maybe I wasn't that ready."

He was held without a shot in the next game at Carolina as the Coyotes were shut out. When the team went to Washington and stayed at the Ritz, Hodgman made sure he enjoyed the experience, opening the closet, putting on the robe, ordering room service for the next morning and enjoying a couple of beverages from the mini fridge. Feeling instinctively this might be his last NHL game, he lived it up a little.

Because the game started at 2 p.m., there was no morning skate, so Hodgeman walked over to the White House. Even though he's Canadian, he enjoyed the history and pageantry of the place.

"I was still so fresh," he said. "I felt like I wasn't going to last so long. The team wasn't playing well, I was a 26-year-old rookie, and there was no time to waste. I wish I would have adapted a little bit quicker and not be so raw for so long. Maybe it would have made a difference and I could have stayed longer."

He was OK early on during the game, even speaking Russian to Alex Ovechkin before a faceoff.

"I just couldn't believe I was lining up against this guy," Hodgman said. "I just said, 'Hey, how are you?' but he didn't respond."

Despite four points from Ovechkin, Washington lost 6-5. Hodgman was held without a shot on goal and was minus-1, sitting out the third period.

"I was definitely tired that game," he said. "I think they probably decided between the second and third period that they were sending me down, so they didn't want to risk me getting injured, because they can't send you down if you get hurt."

After scoring in his first NHL game, Hodgman had no points, one shot on goal and was minus-1 over his next three games. He woke up to a phone call from General Manager Don Maloney telling him he was going back to Portland.

For some reason, Hodgman never played well in Portland that season, scoring 11 goals and 35 points in 62 games. For four months, there wasn't a sniff of getting called back up again, until March 21 when the Coyotes were playing at home against Pittsburgh.

When Hodgman arrived, there was a glass case in his stall commemorating his first game, with the puck from his first goal and pictures of him scoring, celebrating with teammates and holding the first puck, an unbelievably class act by the organization, Hodgman said.

He played 18 shifts in the game on the wing, getting caught out on the ice during an icing against the Penguins' top line, including Sydney Crosby.

"We're taking a faceoff, and I wanted to ask him for an autograph before they drop the puck," Hodgman said with a chuckle. "He's directing things like a general, telling everybody where to go, and I'm like, 'Holy crap! Let's drop the puck!' But he's allowed to do whatever he wants. He's earned it."

So what happens?

"They won the faceoff, his play worked and they scored. I've never been happier on the ice for a goal against. I got that minus against Crosby. I almost wanted to go into their circle. It was like a pitcher giving up a home run to Ken Griffey Jr. You can't be too mad about that. It was a very cool experience."

It was also his last in the NHL as the player he had replaced returned from an injury the next game. Hodgman took the warm-up in the next game against Vancouver but was scratched from the lineup.

"I knew it was pretty much over, it was obvious," he said. "I probably shouldn't even have gotten called up, because I wasn't playing that well in Portland, but I think they were trying to give me a boost before the playoffs. I ended up getting a concussion before the playoffs and not even playing."

Hodgman knew, after his struggles in Portland, it was unlikely he'd get another chance with the Coyotes, but his time with them had set him up for his immediate future. At the very least, he'd have stronger opportunities in Europe, but he signed a one-year deal with St. Louis and its AHL farm team in Chicago.

He knew it would be much tougher to make St. Louis, and he was the first training camp cut. At least playing in Chicago, he'd be closer to Fort Wayne so his family could visit more often.

It should have been a perfect situation, but it just wasn't as Hodgman was limited to six assists in 15 games.

"I got snakebit," he said. "I found out they were going to trade me, which is fine, but if I'm going to be in California or Finland or Sweden, I'm still not going to see the kids. I said, 'If you guys are going to trade me, why don't we just call this good and rip up this deal?' There was no animosity, and I needed a fresh start anyway."

He finished the 2015-16 season in Sweden before playing in the Czech Republic and Finland in 2016-17.

His NHL time might not have been quite what he dreamed of, but Hodgman still made it further than most players.

"I'm still extremely proud about it," he said. "I have no problem talking about how proud I am of the accomplishment. The NHL was a very cool experience."

What he accomplished sunk in a little when, as he was back playing in Europe, fans came up to him after games to ask him to sign his Arizona hockey card.

Longest time between Komets appearances

Player	Time
Bobby Rivard	8 seasons
Peter Sidorkniewicz	8 seasons
Rob Tudor	8 seasons
Justin Hodgman	7 seasons
Konstantin Shafranov	7 seasons
Steve Fletcher	7 seasons
Parris Duffus	7 seasons
Guy Dupuis	6 seasons
Chick Balon	6 seasons
Steve Fletcher	6 seasons
Stephan Brochu	6 seasons
Ed Campbell	6 seasons
Tom Nemeth	6 seasons
Chick Balon	6 seasons
Kelly Hurd	5 seasons
Robin Bawa	5 seasons
Mike Boland	5 seasons
Bob Essensa	5 seasons
Pokey Reddick	5 seasons (twice)

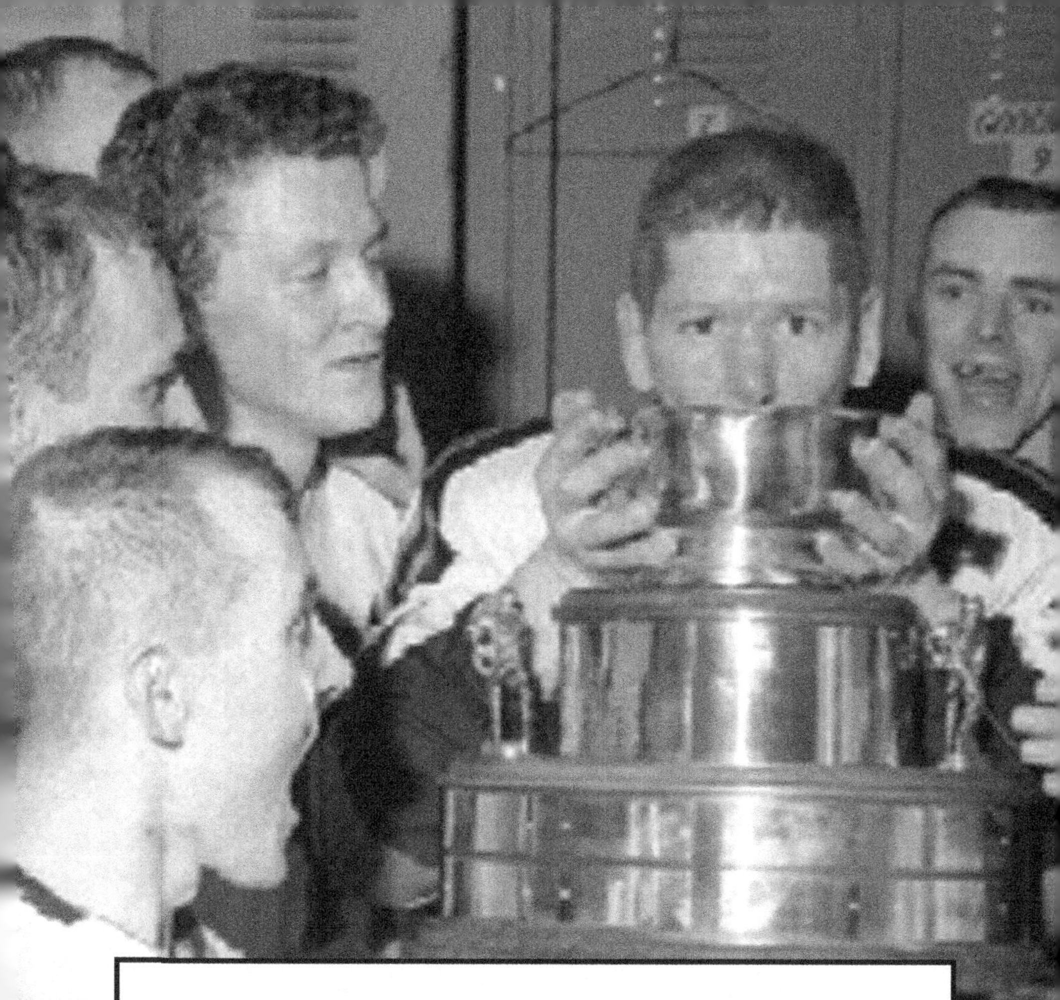

Most championships as a Komets player

Player	Championships
Colin Chaulk	5
Kevin Bertram	4
Nick Boucher	4
Guy Dupuis	4
P.C. Drouin	3
Justin Hodgman	3
David Hukalo	3
Leo Thomas	3
Brandon Warner	3

CHAPTER 42

Reiter found dream job with national team

Since he retired as a Fort Wayne Komet in 2011, Kevin Reiter has traveled the world – and figured out how to make someone else pay for it. He's even turned it into a career opportunity, and it's likely Reiter has a longer, deeper reach into the hockey world than any former Komet, maybe ever.

Reiter, 35, was named USA Hockey's National Team Development Program director of player personnel in August 2017, meaning he's essentially the assistant general manager of U.S. national teams. Everyone from NHL head coaches to college, juniors and international hockey people all return his phone calls or try to get in touch with him to pick his brain on players.

"I love my job," Reiter said. "I love coming to work every day. Everybody is so motivated. There's a lot of travel, but I don't even consider it work. It's a dream job when you see kids have success. God, it's a great feeling."

As a player, Reiter was always one of the more intelligent, hard-working players in any team's locker room. He was friendly, articulate, respected and thoughtful. Everyone on any squad he played for had him slotted in with a big future as a coach.

He started out as a goaltending and assistant coach in Sterzing, Italy, also working in Germany and Austria before he and his wife, Tricia, had a daughter, Alessia. That spurred them to come home, and Reiter became first the goaltending coach and then an assistant coach with the National Team Development

Kevin Reiter
Courtesy of The News-Sentinel

Program in Plymouth, Mich. He was in charge of scouting, recruiting and then developing the goaltenders for every USA team, giving input on teams from 8-year-olds through to the Olympics.

The hours and travel were demanding and constant, but Reiter loved his work, especially getting to know young players and their families and helping them get better. He also had a knack for it.

As an example, he recruited Jake Oettinger out of Minnesota, convincing him to come train in Michigan and become part of the program for two years. That translated into one year at Boston University, and in 2017, Oettinger was a first-round draft pick by the Dallas Stars.

"Coach, there's no way I'd be standing here right now without you and the National Team Development Program," Oettinger told Reiter when he was drafted. "I can't thank you enough for convincing me to come."

Oettinger wasn't just spreading manure.

"The biggest thing for my game when I joined the development program was (goaltending coach) Kevin Reiter," Oettinger told USA Hockey's Mike McMahon in 2016. "For the first time, I had a goalie coach with me every single day. He was always on us to make sure we were getting better, but he was also someone I could talk to like a friend when I was having a problem, and he was really great in making sure we were always developing."

It's Reiter's personality, attention to detail and dedication that attracted USA Hockey to try him in the new position. The last two player personnel directors had taken NHL scouting positions, along with four others in the department. USA Hockey needed someone to provide stability and continuity to the program. They needed someone to make a commitment, and Reiter was ready. He likely would have gotten a goaltending coach position soon in the AHL or NHL, but this is the one he was made for.

"To me, the United States of America is the biggest brand in the world. I didn't have a great idea before this about what the National Team Development Program was or what it was all about," Reiter said. "Once I got involved with it and started working here and seeing the culture and the resources, I knew I wanted to be part of this as long as possible. Before this program was established, we were always underdogs. Now we go into tournaments with the expectations of getting a medal. It's crazy how far we've come in the last 20 years."

And now his biggest job is to organize all the scouts and find the kids who make the best fit for the program. Finding the next potential Jack Eichel, Auston Matthews or Dylan Larkin means convincing players they can't have facial or long hair, they must maintain a stiff grade point average, they will have to move away from home and live with a billet family. What they get in return is the chance to rapidly improve, play against the best competition in the world and have the best resources to work with.

Since it started in 1996, the NTDP has helped more than 250 players get drafted into the NHL, including more than 60 in the first round. And that talent pool continues to increase every year.

"There isn't any better place if you want to develop a new world-class player than in this program," Reiter said. "We have the best resources, the best coaches and the best culture, and it doesn't get any better. The proof is with the amount of players who have come out of here to play in the NHL, play at a high level on international teams and Olympic teams. It's really a special place.

"I'm really passionate about what this place can do for the right player, and I translate that well to them so that they buy in if they want to play at the highest level possible."

Even cooler, if he gets his regular work done, they still let him onto the ice for a few hours each week to scratch his coaching itch.

Maybe Reiter's eventual future will include working on a college for NHL bench or in the front office, but that will come after he's fulfilled his current mission. He's completely dedicated to helping build the national program.

"It's a lot of fun winning medals on foreign soil," he said. "There's no better feeling than standing on the blue line and bending down so someone can put a gold medal around your neck when you're sitting in the middle of Russia or somewhere like that. It's a pretty good feeling."

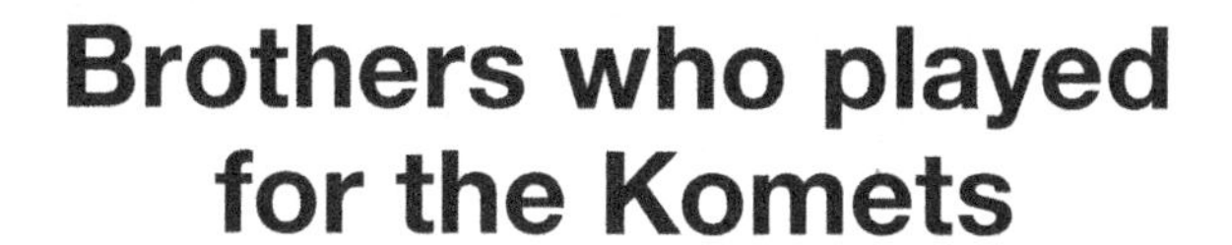

Brothers who played for the Komets

Mike and Neil Buchanan • Edgar and Ken Blondin
Mickey and Jim Shaw • Gerry and Jim Minor
Perry and Paul Pooley • Mark and Steve Salvucci
Sean and Derek Gauthier • Kenny and Kevin Reiter
David and Mikhail Nemirovsky
Bobby and Danny Stewart • Dustin and Bryant Molle
David-Alexandre and Thomas Beauregard

The Buchanans, the Blondins, the Salvuccis, the Pooleys and the Molles played alongside their brother as Komets.

Bob and Bobby Phillips are the only father-son combination.

CHAPTER 43

Bezeau finds new life through hockey

Andy Bezeau
Courtesy of The News-Sentinel

The way Andy Bezeau talks about his early life … well, "I grew up. … I guess the only guy to knock me out was my father. We lived in a house for abused women seven or eight times. Of course you are going to be angry and pissed off after that. How I dealt with it was I fought."

And during a 10-year professional career, Bezeau fought everybody all the time, compiling nearly 4,000 penalty minutes. That's almost 67 games' worth of sitting in the penalty box. During essentially two seasons with the Komets in 1995-96 and 1996-97, Bezeau earned 964 penalty minutes in 127 games.

Though he was only 5 feet 9 and maybe 185 pounds, Bezeau might be the best small fighter in minor league history, especially considering he was always fighting opponents who were significantly larger. With a resume like that, it could be assumed that Bezeau might have ended up in jail or maybe even worse after his career ended in 2000 at age 30.

Instead, he's working in the NHL, mostly because he doesn't fight any more but instead concentrates on the playing side of the game. Bezeau is entering his second season as a scout with the Montreal Canadiens.

He's also become an exceptional youth coach who has developed new techniques to teach skating and movement on the ice. He calls himself a functional movement coach; his protégés have started college careers, and a few have been drafted into the elite junior leagues.

How did all this happen?

For one thing, he got married and his wife, Michelle, helped settle him down. At first, after he retired from playing, he tried to be an underwater welder, but the water pressure at depth was too hard on his joints. Then he joined Michelle's family's roofing company but fell off a roof 45 feet to the driveway. He suffered a grade 2 concussion, a torn rotator cuff, a torn bicep and a cracked pelvis.

"They said if I wasn't in good shape, I would have passed," he said. "I always said it knocked the stupid out of me."

Andy next worked as a brick layer in factories, but when he and Michelle started having kids, he turned back to hockey to find his living, just not the hockey he'd played.

Instead, Bezeau found his own niche by intensely studying the game, down to every detail of what the great players were doing on the ice in every situation. Using video, he broke down their skating movements, charting them so he could essentially dissect their patterns so he could teach younger players to copy them.

"I found out I was better at teaching than I was at playing," he said. "I became a functional movement coach. I do drills based off zone entries or specific movements. There are certain things that high-level athletes do, and they were either taught it at a young age or back in the day they just did it."

As an example, he used to raise his back leg off the ice 24 centimeters while Martin St. Louis raised his 10. Which was going to be the more efficient, quicker skater? As another example, he teaches players how to absorb and avoid checks so they don't get hurt or knocked off-balance.

"Leaving hockey and looking at it from that point of view, I could really pick up what guys were doing. My skill set now is high, and I'm going on 50. It's like a school teacher, the more you teach it, the more know it, and I've become more efficient at teaching younger kids and finding a better way to do it. It's fascinating when you can see the bell go off in their heads and they start to get it. Maybe they can figure it out younger (than I did)."

He now owns his own teaching business, All Pro Hockey. Bezeau thinks functional movement is a teachable skill, but could he have taught himself, say 30 years ago?

"You couldn't talk to that guy," he said with a laugh. "I'm not sure back then I could have absorbed it because I wasn't ready to. Now I can relate to them. I call it proper guidance from a young age. Certain people don't have it or didn't have it. You miss little windows in your career, or you made a bad decision so things didn't work out the way they could have. The way I teach kids, I tell them not to have a door shut on you because of a dumb decision.

"A regret I have is that maybe if I had changed my thought process, things could have been better quicker. I don't want kids to have the regrets I had."

He made himself into a hockey mind, and the things he learned helped make the transition to scouting easy. The Canadiens reached out to Bezeau a couple of years ago and asked if he'd be interested, testing him and giving him a few assignments before offering a position in the organization. He watched 250 games last season, and that doesn't count the ones on TV or if he went to a youth game.

"I didn't make it to the NHL as a player, but I'm there now," he said. "You're in discussions that help make people millionaires. It's kind of interesting from that point of view."

Because of his new skills, Bezeau said he's thinking about branching into professional coaching sometime within the next few years. He believes he can help pro players improve through video and on-ice work. He thinks the timing might be right, especially with the way the game has changed.

"When I first started, people were always saying, 'You're a goon,' but you don't ever hear that now," Bezeau said. "Kids don't have to put up with that anymore because it doesn't happen. Today, now you just play. You don't have to worry about fighting."

Most penalty minutes in a season

1. Andy Bezeau 1995-96 590
2. Sean Gagnon 1996-97.................... 457
3. Kevin Kaminski 1990-91 455
4. Chris McRae 1991-92 413
5. Andre Roy 1998-99 395
6. Robin Bawa 1990-91 381
7. Jeff Worlton 2004-05 372
8. Steve Fletcher 1992-93 337
9. Steve Fletcher 1991-92 320
9. Andy Bezeau 1996-97 320
11. Carl Mokosak 1989-90.................... 315
12. Kevin Kotyluk 2003-04.................... 313
13. Bruce Shoebottom 1986-87 309
14. Shawn Penn 1998-99...................... 308
15. Dale Baldwin 1984-85 297
15. Mitch Woods 2007-08 297
17. Robbie Laird 1978-79 296
17. Mike Lekun 1987-88 296
19. Scott Gruhl 1992-93....................... 290
20. Steve Fletcher 1990-91 289

CHAPTER 44
Fort Wayne's Russian Revolution

You're 22 years old and your job just sent you overseas. You don't know the language, you'll be going alone and you won't know anyone there. You can't even count on the job being very stable because you can be transferred with little notice. Luckily, you're not married, or you'd also be separated from your spouse.

That's pretty much the scenario Russian hockey players faced when they came to North America during the early 1990s. It was also rare for any countrymen to be on the same team, and no one else spoke the language. The individual players were truly alone.

Luckily, hockey is an international language, and the sport helped the immigrant players adjust quickly. Fort Wayne became a minor league hotbed of adopting Russian players. Because the Komets were a small-market team competing in the International Hockey League during the 1990s, they could not hope to compete against the high-salary teams such as Las Vegas, Detroit, Chicago, San Diego or Orlando.

The Komets needed to find a cheaper way to be competitive, and they found it by recruiting Russian players who were desperate for a North American place to play so they could show off for NHL scouts. Hypothetically, the Komets could sign a Russian player for, say, $75,000 who had the skill level of a North American player who could demand more than $100,000 for an IHL season. The Russians, especially the forwards, provided the Komets with high-level skilled players who allowed them to compete.

Since Igor Chibirev in 1992, the Komets have become masters at helping Russians feel comfortable, and the Russian players have helped the Komets remain a competitive team in the expanding International Hockey League. The Russians want to play in North America because that's where they can make a good living doing what they love.

Since Chibirev broke the international barrier by coming to Fort Wayne in 1992, Vladimir Tsyplakov, Konstantin Shafranov, Andrei Bashkirov and Viacheslav Butsayev all parlayed big years with the Komets into National Hockey League contracts.

"There are a lot of coaches who try to make the Russians into North American players," Komets General Manager David Franke said. "They are not known for physical play, but there are a lot of coaches who try to demand that style of play out of them. Consequently, they don't think they are very good players."

The Komets helped the players transition with the help of translator Boris Zinchenko, a Ukraine native who moved to Fort Wayne in 1949 and was retired from International Harvester. He helped the players find apartments and apply for driver's licenses, and he co-signed for phone bills and leads – things almost all Americans take for granted.

When Chibirev became the first Russian Komet, he did not know three words of English, but Zinchenko helped him find an English teacher.

Igor Chibirev

Courtesy of The News-Sentinel

"When he came in, he was all by himself," said Chibirev's teammate, Paul Willett. "We wondered what he did all day, because it has to be tough. Now the players who have come over before really help the new guys out."

The hardest part is learning the language and communicating with teammates on the ice.

"When you are on the ice, hockey is hockey, and we didn't talk that much," Willett said. "Then we'd come back to the bench, and every now and then, we'd use sign language."

Although most Russian players would rather drop their gloves and fight on the ice than talk to American reporters, they quickly pick up the basics of the English language. They usually understand more than they speak, and there are few players who do not adapt.

The language situation also has led to some funny stories.

During a 1994 playoff game against Peoria, Tsyplakov skated to the penalty box with a two-minute slashing penalty. As he sat in the box, the Peoria fans around the box screamed every profanity they could think of at Tsyplakov, who ignored them without a glance.

After his penalty ended and Tsyplakov skated back onto the ice, the penalty box attendant turned to someone sitting in the box and said, "Don't these idiots get it that he can't understand them?"

One day, Chibirev was watching a movie in the dressing room when one character in the show suggested another try something that was anatomically impossible. Not understanding, Chibirev asked a teammate, "How you (bleep) yourself?"

Helpfully, his teammates kept saying he should go ask the next person.

"A lot of times, they can understand it better than they can talk it," Franke said. "Sometimes the coaches thought they could talk English a lot better than they did, and that sometimes led to problems. You would also see a difference when they would go back to Russia for the summer, and the next fall, it would seem like they had to pick it up all over again."

Some of their teammates also wondered how well the players really understood English. Numerous times during practice a few years ago, the members of the "MiG line" – Butsayev, Shafranov and Bashkirov – would act differently on and off the ice.

"It always amazed me how the coach could be trying to tell them something on the ice in English, and they wouldn't understand a word he was saying," retired former Komet Robin Bawa said. "As soon as we got into the locker room and started talking about money, they understood everything down to the last penny. They understood perfectly when it came to getting paid. They always spoke perfect English in bars, too."

Vadim Sharapov played junior hockey in North America before joining the Komets.

"Once in juniors, we had a team meeting, and I heard a word that sounded like 'prostitution,'" Sharapov said. "The coach was actually talking about property, but I asked the guy sitting next to me, 'Was he talking about prostitution?' And this guy tells the coach I had a question about prostitution."

Non-North American countries whose players have been Komets

Belarus • Czech Republic • England • Finland
Holland • Italy • Kazakhstan • Latvia • Netherlands
New Zealand • Poland • Romania • Russia
Scotland • Slovakia • Sweden • Uganda • Ukraine

CHAPTER 45

MiG line provided Komets with unbelievable memories

Ever since the Komets brought Igor Chibirev over in 1992 and signed Vladimir Tsyplakov and Igor Malykhin in 1993, Komets General Manager David Franke had a dream of putting together a Russian line. He even acquired Oleg Mikulchik, Mikhail Nemirovsky, Yuri Krivokhija, Sergei Stas, Nikolai Tsulygin, Igor Nikulin and Ravil Yakubov during the 1996-97 season, but the Komets suffered through their worst season, going 28-47-7.

As one of the International Hockey League's smaller markets, Fort Wayne could not afford to compete with teams such as Detroit, Chicago, Las Vegas or Orlando, which were willing to pay more than $2 million in player salaries. With a payroll of around $1 million, the Komets needed a shortcut, and Franke thought he found one when he signed Viacheslav Butsayev and Konstantin Shafranov in the summer of 1997.

Though they had the skills of major IHL stars, the Russians did not command the higher salaries.

It turned out Shafranov and Butsayev were not enough. On Nov. 21, the Komets were 6-10-1 and holding last place in the league.

They were scoring a league-low 2.88 goals per game and giving up a second-worst 3.47 goals per game. Though many IHL executives scoffed, Franke decided to go even more Russian, acquiring winger Andrei Bashkirov from Las Vegas for future considerations.

Named after a series of Russian fighter planes, the 'MiG line' was finally formed.

And the Komets took off immediately, going 19-5-3 in "the burst from worst to first," winning 11 straight games at one point to take over the division lead. During a 15-game stretch, there were only two times members of the MiG line were held without a point, as they combined for 17 goals and 47 points.

"Sometimes you can just get them the puck, and they can make magic," Komets defenseman Chris Armstrong said.

The trio's play was creative, artistic and graceful, something never seen in North American minor league hockey. Twice Butsayev scored goals from near the blue line by snapping shots on net without turning his head as everyone on the ice was expecting him to pass.

"I didn't look," Butsayev said. "I just made the decision to shoot, and sometimes good things happen."

The season's most beautiful goal happened in Indianapolis. From deep inside his own blue line, Butsayev hit Bashkirov at the red line with a perfect 40-foot backhand saucer pass, and Bashkirov then set up Shafranov with another perfect 40-foot saucer pass to leave Ice goaltender Marc Lamothe befuddled as Shafranov scored easily.

"That one line, when they are going, they are fun to watch as a spectator, but as an opposing coach it's not a whole lot of fun," Indianapolis coach Bob Ferguson said.

The MiG Line
Courtesy of The News-Sentinel

They toyed with opposing defenses, scoring 92 goals, though only 16 were on the power play. That led to some outrageous plus-minus numbers as Shafranov was plus-39, Butsayev plus-42 and Bashkirov plus-49 to lead the league. They skated too well to hit and always moved the puck before baffled defensemen could react.

"They're the closest thing to NHL players and an NHL line in this league for sure," Cincinnati coach Ron Smith said. "You could take them right now and move them up. ... They're a treat and good for the league."

Butsayev finished with 86 points, Shafranov 80 and Bashkirov 76 as the Komets tied the biggest season-to-season turnaround in franchise history, improving from 63 points to 100. Franke was named the IHL's General Manager of the Year for the second time, and John Torchetti was named IHL Coach of the Year.

After losing in the first round of the playoffs, the Komets tried to re-sign all three, but Bashkirov was drafted by Montreal, and Shafranov left to play in his native Kazakhstan. Though signed by Florida and then dealt to Ottawa, Butsayev came back to lead the Komets in scoring with 72 points in 71 games, and Bashkirov scored 36 points in 34 games after Montreal sent him down.

Despite trying several European players, the Komets could not find a winger to replace Shafranov. He finally came back for the playoffs, but by then, Bashkirov was up with Montreal so the MiG line was never re-formed.

The 1998-99 season was also the Komets' last in the original

IHL, as they moved to the United Hockey League in 1999-2000. The IHL spent itself into oblivion in 2000-01.

Today, Shafranov is coaching in Russia, Butsayev coaches in Russia's Kontinental Hockey League and Bashkirov has retired to Switzerland.

Russians who have played for the Komets

** Signed NHL contracts after playing with the Komets*

*Igor Chibirev 1992-93, 1994-95

Igor Ulanov 1992-93

*Vladimir Tsyplakov 1993-94, 1994-95

Igor Malykhin 1993-94, 1994-95, 1999-2000, 2000-01

*Konstantin Shafranov 1995-96, 1997-98, 1998-99, 1999-2000, 2007-08, 2008-09, 2009-10

Andrei Mezin 1995-96

Oleg Yashin 1995-96

Sergei Stas 1995-96, 1996-97

Oleg Mikoulchik 1996-97

Igor Nikulin 1996-97

Mikhail Nemirovsky 1996-97

Nikolai Tsulygin 1996-97, 1998-99

Ravil Yakubov 1996-97

*Viacheslav Butsayev 1997-98, 1998-99

*Andrei Bashkirov 1997-98, 1998-99

Roman Oksiuta 1997-98

Andrei Petrakov 1998-99

Oleg Shagorodsky 1998-99

Andrei Sryubko 1998-99

Vadim Sharapov 1999-2000

Alex Mukanov 1999-2000

Anton Pavlychev 1999-2000

Evgeny Tsybuk 1999-2000

Konstantin Simchuk 2000-01

Igor Bonderev 2001-02

Evgeny Saidachev 2007-08, 2008-09, 2009-10

Artem Podshendyalov 2010-11, 2011-12

Andrey Makarov 2013-14

Nakita Kashirsky 2015-16

CHAPTER 46

Weekes carries work ethic into broadcasting

During his 14-year professional hockey career, Kevin Weekes was always articulate and intelligent, never ducked a question and always gave thoughtful answers. Communicating is what he did second-best to frustrating shooters.

As a player, he needed a break to prove what he could do and to earn a spot in the NHL. The same thing was true when he finished playing in 2009 and decided that he wanted a broadcasting career.

Weekes was a raw 22-year-old full of potential when he came to the Komets in 1997-98 as a Florida Panthers prospect. The Panthers had John Vanbiesbrouck and Mark Fitzpatrick and no room for Weekes on their roster. Yet.

"I remember (Panthers General Manager) Bryan Murray telling me he knew I was close, but I needed to go to the IHL and dominate, and if I did that, he'd create a spot for me," Weekes said. "My dad and I drove from Toronto to Fort Wayne, and I started to feel comfortable. I loved the rink, and the fans were so passionate. The guys on the team were so cool to me and accommodating. It was really a perfect situation."

Weekes went 9-2-1 with a 2.84 goals-against average and .918 save percentage as a Komet. He did everything Murray asked. During late December, he made 36 saves to win 1-0 at Grand Rapids. A few nights later, the Komets played at Detroit, a place they had always struggled against the Vipers.

"I remember just telling the guys that it didn't matter what happened, we just had to get three goals because Weeksie was not going to give anything up," Komets coach John Torchetti said. "I told (assistant coach Grant Sonier) this guy is going to hold the fort all night long for us."

Weekes made 43 saves to win 4-3. He consistently found ways to make what seemed to be impossible saves and take the breath out of a Palace of Auburn Hills crowd of 17,254.
A few days later, Weekes was recalled to Florida and never came back. The next year, he had a contract dispute with the Panthers and played for the Vipers before being traded to Vancouver. He never played in the minors again.

"I have always said that Fort Wayne had a big hand in getting me to the NHL at a critical time for me," Weekes said. "John Torchetti, Robin Bawa, Ian Boyce, Joe Franke, Racer, the Frankes, all those guys were so good to me. They just treated me so well."

Weekes stayed in the NHL two years with Vancouver, one with the Islanders and two with Tampa Bay before having his best two seasons with Carolina. He helped the Hurricanes reach the 2002 Stanley Cup Finals, where they lost to the Red Wings in five games.

His playing career finished with two years playing for the Rangers and then a final two seasons with New Jersey. Then he needed someone to give him another chance.

"In playing, I think I was always comfortable in front of the camera, even when I was younger and going back to my early teams," Weekes said. "As I got a little bit on in my hockey career, because I was comfortable on the camera and on the mic, I guess subconsciously I kind of thought about (broadcasting) and entertained it, and I started doing some different things at ESPN and different TV opportunities."

What Weekes doesn't mention is that in 2009 at 34, he became the first black analyst, joining Hockey Night in Canada. He's worked for Madison Square Garden's network, NBC and now The NHL Network, where he's on air 200 days a year.

Almost as rare, he's a former goaltender giving his insight into the game.

"I think it does make a difference," he said. "It's pretty similar to playing quarterback or catching in that it's kind of an individualized position within a team sport. When you are playing goal, 95 percent of the game is played in front of us. We're constantly reading, reacting, calculating, processing, evaluating.

"With all those plays developing in front of us, around us, beside us and the odd one behind us, it offers a real unique vantage point. There's the accountability as well, and that unique first-person perspective to see so much of the play in front of you. I'm very detail-oriented , just picking out little things as goalies, like where the shooter's hands are on the stick, is the blade open, are his hands a little more closed, anticipating where other players are and who may be open. There's a lot to discern in a short amount of time as a goalie, and that helps me as a broadcaster."

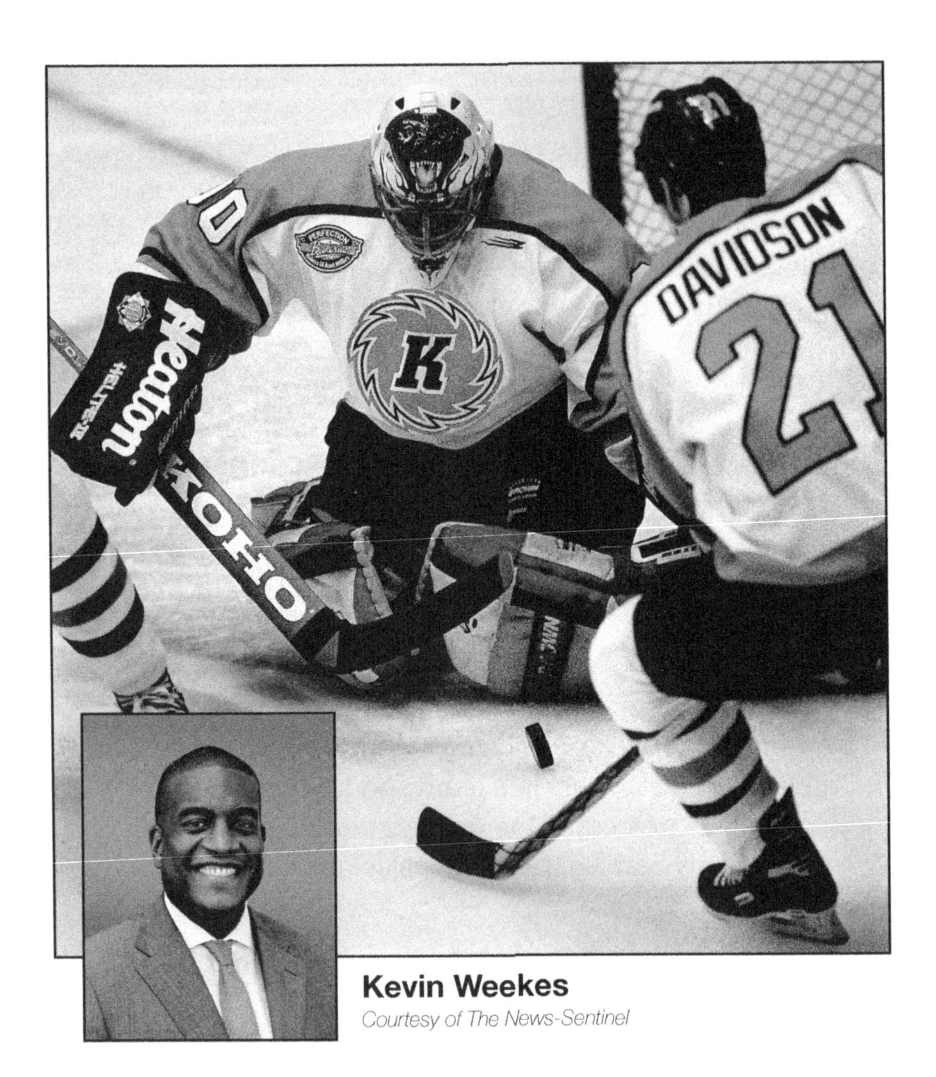

Kevin Weekes
Courtesy of The News-Sentinel

But Weekes doesn't just rely on his playing days to inform his analysis. The work ethic he developed as a player continues to drive him to improve. His phone is constantly ringing, and Weekes talks with people at all levels and professions in the sport. He's still hungry to learn and to grow.

"I love it. I have a lot of fun broadcasting, and I feel I owe it to the NHL viewer and the fans to be insightful, dialed in and (as) factual as possible," he said. "I love the challenge of it, I love working and I love grinding. This is a great game to be a part of, and every day I feel compelled to earn that right. I never feel as though I've arrived or I'm complacent. Any time I go on the air or do social media, I'm driving to be as successful and do the best I can for our team."

That's part of the sacrifice he learned from his parents, who emigrated from Barbados to Toronto, and Weekes continues to raise funds for youth charities in both areas, partly through his No5Hole clothing brand.

But it all really started in Fort Wayne.

CHAPTER 47

Bowman provides perspective on Komets

Scotty Bowman
Courtesy of Chicago Blackahawks

Almost every year since 2004, a special person usually shows up during the Christmas holidays to watch a Komets game at Memorial Coliseum. No, it's not Santa Claus. It's somebody better than that.

Since his daughter Alicia's family moved to Fort Wayne in 2004, NHL coaching great Scotty Bowman has become a semi-regular visitor to the city, especially to see his two granddaughters.

"Every time I see him, he'll say, 'I was back in Fort Wayne,'" said Auburn native and former Chicago Blackhawks Senior Director of Communications and Community Relations Brandon Faber. "He loves going to the Komets games."

The most successful coach in NHL history, Bowman won nine Stanley Cup titles with Montreal, Pittsburgh and Detroit and five others as a front-office member. He's currently a senior advisor of hockey operations for the Blackhawks.

And he comes to Fort Wayne about four times a year.

"It's a good hockey city," Bowman said. "It's got a lot of tradition. They've lasted all this time. They always seem to have competitive teams, a good core of people and a hockey culture in Fort Wayne."

He's not just saying that for the public relations value. Bowman actually knows a great deal about the Komets, more than just a casual hockey fan.

He played in juniors with all-time Fort Wayne leading scorer Len Thornson, and he coached former Komets goaltenders Chuck Adamson and Gerry Randall in juniors and Robbie Irons with the St. Louis Blues. He knew late Komets coach Ken Ullyot and players Reggie Primeau and Lionel Repka. He also knows Mr. Komet Eddie Long from Ottawa.

"I have been involved in hockey since 1956 full time, but even before that, you could always listen to Bob Chase and the Komets games on the radio from WOWO," Bowman said. "They came in very loud and clear into Canada. I lived in Montreal, and we could get the games just like a local broadcast."

Bowman can talk about former Fort Wayne NHL players Fred Knipscheer and Dale Purinton. He knows all about the Zollner Pistons basketball teams, which moved to Detroit in 1957.

Bowman also knows Los Angeles Kings scout and former Komets player and coach Rob Laird, and he respects that Laird gave up his spot on the 2014 Stanley Cup so that someone else's name could be engraved on it.

"He's just a nice guy," Bowman said.

Bowman can and will talk any era in any league, even the minors. He also met Wolcottville native Karch Bachman at a USA Hockey Developmental Camp in Buffalo in 2014. Bachman, a Florida Panthers prospect, plays at Miami of Ohio.

Along with going to his first Komets game in October 2004, Bowman was interviewed a couple of times by Bob Chase, whom he had met as coach of the St. Louis Blues in 1968.

"We didn't have an announcer, so the second year, we were trying to get somebody to come in, and the guy the owner focused on was Bob Chase," Bowman said. "Bob was supposed to go to St. Louis and do an audition for the owner, but there was a big basketball tournament the same weekend and he didn't go."

Chase got a late call on Friday afternoon to come to St. Louis but was already committed to broadcasting the IHSAA state tournament on WOWO. He didn't think he could renege.

"He was just a wonderful guy," Bowman said.

A few years ago, Bowman went to lunch with Ullyot and Thornson when Ullyot told him a story about the Canadiens coming to Fort Wayne for exhibition games against the Komets in 1962 and 1963. Despite former Komet John Ferguson playing with the Canadiens in the second game, the crowd was only 2,422 fans on a Tuesday night.

"What Ken Ullyot said was the game was not a success for whatever reason," Bowman recalled. "The Canadiens were supposed to get a percentage of the box office, and when he went to pay (Montreal coach) Toe Blake, Blake said, 'No, you didn't make enough money here,' and he wouldn't take any money."

Blake Siebenaler
Courtesy of Niagara IceDogs

Bowman said he's surprised there haven't been more hockey players from Fort Wayne make it to the NHL. Knipscheer and Purinton are the only ones, though Bachman and Columbus Blue Jackets prospect Blake Siebenaler have a chance.

"There should have been more of them, though, because the popularity of the Komets should have spilled over," Bowman said. "It's kind of odd to me why the youth hockey didn't catch on as much. Maybe there was a lack of ice available or something."

That certainly was a big reason for decades, though there have been 11 Fort Wayne players who grew up to play for the Komets.

Bowman lives in Sarasota, Fla., with his wife, Suella. He goes to all the Tampa Bay Lightning home games to scout for the Blackhawks (his son is Chicago's general manager), and occasionally, he'll go to an ECHL Florida Everblades game in Estero. He also stays up late watching the West Coast games on TV.

And of course he looks forward to coming back to Fort Wayne to see granddaughters Ashley and Lindsay and also the Komets.

"It's a nice rink that has stood the test of time," Bowman said. "It was way ahead of its time when it was built. I appreciate that I can sit up in the stands, and the fans don't bother me much. I like the hockey."

ABOUT THE AUTHOR

Blake Sebring

Blake Sebring began working for The News-Sentinel as a high school sophomore and started as a full-timer in 1988. After the legendary Bud Gallmeier retired in 1990, Sebring took over coverage of the Fort Wayne Komets, the second-oldest minor league team in North America.

He is the author of nine books and was inducted into the Indiana Sportswriters and Sportscasters Association Hall of Fame in 2015.

His hockey work can be followed at news-sentinel.com, and his books are available at blakesebring.com and on Amazon.

Made in the USA
Monee, IL
22 December 2021